D0254202

NATIONS AND STATES
IN SOUTHEAST ASIA

This reflective and provocative book outlines the emergence of the nation-states of modern Southeast Asia. It considers various ways of looking at Southeast Asian history, combining narrative, analysis and discussion. The book focuses mainly on the period from the eighteenth century to the present. It is divided into three sections: the first gives a broad historical overview of Indonesia, Malaysia, Singapore, Brunei, The Philippines, Burma/Myanmar, Vietnam and Siam/Thailand; the second reflects, in a comparative context, on significant problems in understanding Southeast Asia's past and present; the third explores the current state of writing Southeast Asian history. Underlying the discussion is an awareness of how ongoing tensions between East and West shape history and frame the present. This book reflects a lifetime's scholarship and will become a major interpretative synthesis of modern Southeast Asia.

Nicholas Tarling was Professor of History at the University of Auckland from 1968 to 1997. He edited the two-volume *Cambridge History of Southeast Asia*, published in 1992, and wrote *Britain, Southeast Asia and the Onset of the Pacific War*, published by Cambridge in 1996. He was the founder president of the New Zealand Asian Studies Society and is currently a Fellow of the New Zealand Asia Institute at the University of Auckland.

MMkisk777

NATIONS AND STATES IN SOUTHEAST ASIA

Nicholas Tarling

CAMBRIDGE
UNIVERSITY PRESS

PUBLISHED BY THE PRESS SYNDICATE OF THE UNIVERSITY OF CAMBRIDGE
The Pitt Building, Trumpington Street, Cambridge, United Kingdom

CAMBRIDGE UNIVERSITY PRESS
The Edinburgh Building, Cambridge CB2 2RU, UK http://www.cup.cam.ac.uk
40 West 20th Street, New York, NY 10011–4211, USA http://www.cup.org
10 Stamford Road, Oakleigh, Melbourne 3166, Australia

First published 1998

Printed in Hong Kong by Colorcraft Ltd.

Typeset in Sabon 10/12 pt

A catalogue record for this book is available from the British Library

Library of Congress Cataloguing in Publication data

Tarling, Nicholas.
Nations and states in Southeast Asia/Nicholas Tarling.
    p.   cm.
Includes bibliographical references and index.
ISBN 0-521-62245-X (hc: alk. paper). – ISBN 0-521-62564-5 (pbk: alk. paper)
1. Asia, Southeastern – History – 1945– . 2. Asia, Southeastern –
Historiography. 3. Nationalism – Asia, Southeastern – History.
4. National State. I. Title.
DS526.7.T36 1998
959.05'3–dc21   97-29973

CONTENTS

For Brook Barrington

PREFACE

The present world is a world of states, neither a world of tribes nor a world of empires, though the remnants of such forms are still present and occupy part of our thinking. Such states, moreover, are based on a concept of nation, though, while states are expected or assumed to be nation-states, not all nations are represented in the world by states, despite widespread aspiration. That world, clearly still emerging, has been emerging over a long period. To a large extent it represents the world-wide application of a European approach to the organisation of human society, though the approach took time to develop even in Europe, and is still indeed in process of application there, too.

One purpose of this book is to outline the emergence of the nation-states of modern Southeast Asia. That is the task of Part One. It can indeed be no more than an outline: and other sources will be needed by those who want to study their history more deeply. Another constraint, less obvious, should also become apparent. In most of Southeast Asia there were states well before the emergence of the system of states with which we are more familiar. They are not, however, the same. In studying the states, we cannot presume that they always existed, or that they were bound to emerge in the ways they have. A summary risks foreshortening the process, allowing the present to dominate the past, offering what Herbert Butterfield would have recognised as a Whig interpretation. 'The theory that is behind the whig interpretation – the theory that we study the past for the sake of the present – is one that is really introduced for the purpose of facilitating the abridgment of history...it serves to simplify the study of history by providing an excuse for leaving things out.'[1]

Part Two of the book takes up some of the issues that arise. But it has another focus, too. The first part of the book attempts to look at the countries as they have emerged one by one, even though that risks the presumptions of 'presentism', that what now exists was bound to exist. The second half of the book represents a more regional focus. So many of the issues are common to each country, yet affected the countries differently. That should make for a better understanding of issues and countries.

Part Two has another rationale as well. In shifting the focus from country to region, it is not only attempting to explain each country's history better: it is also responding to a current interest in Southeast Asia as a region. The concept is indeed in some sense itself quite a modern one. In previous centuries, there were words that attempted to describe it despite its diversity by suggesting some common feature, like 'Further India' or the 'Nanyang'. The term 'Southeast Asia' is more recent, and though it originates in the Second World War, it has tended to gain acceptance. The fact that in yet more recent times the area has become noted for rapid economic advance has added to the currency of the term, even though that advance is in fact highly differentiated.

The extent to which the world has become a world of states has encouraged a tendency to group the states by regions, and sometimes those states have grouped themselves, though always partly in order to attain their objectives as states. 'Southeast Asia' was once a term used by outsiders far more than by those living in the region; but now it is becoming something of an economic and political reality, and its leaders themselves are moving to make ASEAN an organisation of and for the region, instead of an organisation designed to add to the security of some of its states vis-a-vis others. The degree to which supra-state organisations will come to dominate economic and political relations among states remains to be seen. To a large extent they still represent attempts by states to seek their particular interests. States join one or more groups and seek to affect the character of world-wide organisations and their programmes.

Such organisations are an illustration of the extent to which the world has become one at the same time as it has become divided among states of equal sovereignty but different strength. There are, of course, many others. It is a world of 'multinationals' as well as of international relations: successors, say, to the United East India Company of the Dutch, the VOC (Vereenigde Oost-Indische Compagnie), to the English or the Danish East India Companies. Indeed, the striking feature of the discourse of the late twentieth century is its world-wide character. What we argue about is not whether there should be 'democracy' but what kind of democracy it should be; not whether there are 'human rights' but what they are, how they should be applied, and by whom.

This wider discourse also leads to a kind of ideological regionalisation that parallels but is not identical with the geographical, and, like it, may or may not be taken up by nations and their leaders. In some cases, they have again gained pseudo-geographical names, such as the North–South dichotomy, overlapping the other antinomies, like 'developed' and 'underdeveloped'. The more venerable East–West polarity overlapped a similar antinomy, also described as between the 'imperialist' and the 'colonial', the 'developed' and the 'developing'. Given that the world that has taken shape is so deeply affected by the European mode of discourse that has continued to emerge, that is not surprising, particularly as that European mode was taken up, albeit in new focus, by the two most powerful successor-states, the

US and Russia. Just because we have now to look at the world as a whole, we tend to break it up into manageable chunks that may lead us to misinterpret it just as much as the problem of managing chronology contributed to the Whig interpretation of history. Edward Said has given new meaning, but also new currency, to 'Orientalism'. Such interpretations can be useful in modifying mind-sets, but they must not merely replace them. The third part of this book discusses some of the ways of looking at Southeast Asian history.

Southeast Asia, and to a differing extent the countries within it, have witnessed the interplay, often characterised as that between East and West, that in some sense has created the modern world. Now the countries of Southeast Asia reckon the levels of 'development' against the 'international' norms, their own 'multinationals' invest elsewhere, and they proffer their own interpretation of 'human rights'. In a sense this is part of a continuing history, which the three parts of this small volume attempt in modest measure to encompass, through the narratives in Part One, the analyses in Part Two, and the discussion in Part Three.

Tackling this book, the reader may wish to start with the narratives, even perhaps to diverge, on concluding them, and follow up the history of one or more countries in greater depth or detail. With or without that reinforcement, the reader may, the author hopes, want to take up the topics that he has himself found particularly interesting as a result of a long period of study of and teaching about Southeast Asia that has turned out to coincide with a transformation of its place in the world, and of the countries within it. How the rest of the world, itself changing, may understand that change, and in so doing, indeed, contribute to it, is the subject of the concluding remarks. ●

---

1   H. Butterfield, *The Whig Interpretation of History*, London: Bell, 1931, p. 24.

SOUTHEAST ASIA

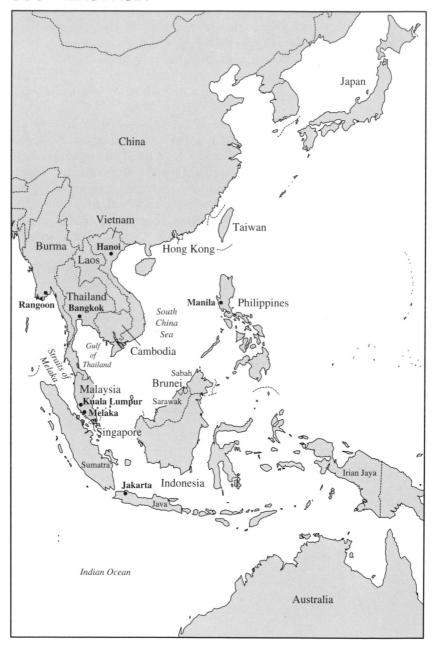

Map of the region, showing present-day national frontiers

Part One

PRESENT AND PAST

This part of the book outlines the emergence of the main countries of modern Southeast Asia. Those in the island part of Southeast Asia – Indonesia, Malaysia, Singapore, Brunei, and the Philippines – are considered first, then those of the mainland, in particular Burma, Vietnam and Thailand. The continuities, it may be argued, are greater in the case of the latter group than in the case of the former, but there are both continuity and discontinuity in all cases. Nor is their history merely a differentiated working-out of the relationship of East and West. It is longer and far more complicated. In these summaries, the focus is on their previous history, on their relations with Europe, on nationalism, and on the establishment and character of the independent states after the Second World War.

INDONESIA

Indonesia has a long history, and a long history of connection with the rest of the world, but not as the state of Indonesia. The ancient states of the archipelago are known to us as a result of records, often Chinese, and of inscriptions and monuments, like those in central Java. The work of historians, in particular Georges Coedès and O. W. Wolters, has recalled the kingdom of Sri Vijaya, which seems to have centred in the region of Palembang from the late eighth century CE. States also emerged in Java, the greatest of which was to be the Majapahit empire, which flourished in the fifteenth century CE. Though its influence was considerable and its political ambit wide, it did not extend over all present-day Indonesia. But its existence was an inspiration to Indonesian nationalists, such as Sukarno.[1]

In the sixteenth century the world became one, though only through European expansion, and as a result it was shaped in part by European power and aspiration. The Portuguese and Spanish voyages 'first made humanity conscious however dimly, of its essential unity'.[2] The Indonesian islands were drawn into that world by the Portuguese, the Dutch, the Spaniards, and the English, and also by others, Indonesians and Chinese, who reacted to them or utilised the opportunities that were opened up. Among the Europeans, the Dutch made themselves dominant during the seventeenth century CE. They founded Batavia in 1619, secured Melaka in 1641, conquered parts of Maluku, the spice islands, and during the succeeding century and a half extended their control over much of Java. But they were not attempting to build an Indonesian state. There were other centres of economic and political activity in the archipelago. Those they did not eliminate, though they often involved other rulers in commercial treaties and contracts. Furthermore, their network of possessions and treaties did not extend merely to the archipelago. Batavia was not the capital of an Indonesian realm. It was the centre of the Asia-wide activities of the VOC, extending from the Persian Gulf to Japan, with settlements on the Indian sub-continent as well as in the archipelago, and with a remote outpost in Nagasaki harbour.

In face of changing economic and political conditions, and of rivalry from the British, the Dutch began in the eighteenth century to focus more on their expanding realm in Java, for which Melaka increasingly became an outpost. That is evident, for example, with the activities of Governor-General van

Imhoff. But it was only in the early nineteenth century that the Dutch set about building a state they called Netherlands India. The old company had finally been terminated in 1799. During the French wars, the restructuring of the state at home was paralleled by attempts to restructure what became its possessions abroad. Napoleon's brother was put on a new throne, and Governor-General Daendels sought to re-make Java in preparation to resist a British invasion. The defeat of Napoleon in 1814–15 led in France to the restoration of the Bourbon monarchy. In the Netherlands, initially expanded to include the Belgian provinces as well as the old Dutch Republic, a new monarchy was created, the Orange princes who had been hereditary Stadhouders of the Republic now becoming kings. A Commission-General was sent out to the Indies.

Even now, though the Dutch shed their possessions on the sub-continent, their possessions in the Indies were not an integrated whole. Nor was the relationship with the metropolis yet clear: in some sense it was formally colonial, in another the islands were an appanage of the monarchy. Both these factors affected the development of the relationship of the archipelago with the rest of the world. Concentrating on the islands after their losses in India, the Dutch concentrated on Java in particular: their claims in other parts of their archipelago often rested, as in the Company's time, on contracts with the rulers, and were seldom backed up by formal possession. The aim, indeed, was still to profit, rather than to rule. The relationship between this entity, or collection of entities, and the metropolis also reflected that. And the relationship with other powers was affected by their readiness to accept Dutch claims, the ability of the Dutch to enforce them, and the Indonesian rulers' ability to sustain their independence in such a situation. In general the creation of Netherlands India was still very much in process. 'The war against the Rajas of Bali' in the 1840s 'was in many ways an uncharacteristic occurrence, a deviation from the general non-interventionist line'.[3] But, slow though it might be, the process did involve a loss of international personality on the part of the Indonesian states. By 1848 only a few were, as the Europeans would say, de jure independent of the Dutch, though many were de facto independent. One of the former was the sultanate of Aceh. Even after the three-stage war with Bali, the Dutch did not at first install a regular administration.

The Belgian revolution of 1830 had deprived the Orange monarchy of its southern provinces, though King Willem I refused for the greater part of a decade to accept the outcome. The year 1848, one of European revolution, did not overthrow the monarchy, but it challenged the Dutch state, and in turn brought changes to the Indies. It encouraged new attempts to round out the realm inasmuch as it opened the way to an emergent Dutch capitalism. At the same time, the Netherlands States-General gained a role in the governance of the Indies, from which it had hitherto been excluded.

Governments had acted till then, as Sloet tot Oldhuis put it, as if 'the colonies did not concern the Nation and consequently should lie outside its circle of cognizance, like a sort of crown domain'.[4] Coupled, therefore, with capitalist penetration, there was an attempt to assert a public responsibility for the empire. That might mean more extensive and more intrusive government; it might also mean a more accountable form of government. Changes in one term of the series affected the other two. The realm, increasingly described as, for example in the Agrarian Law of 1870, a 'state',[5] became more integrated. At the same time its relationship with the outside world became more explicitly and more completely colonial. After a prolonged struggle Aceh lost its independence. So did Bali and Lombok. Though the realm yet remained a congeries of directly and indirectly ruled territories – there were 288 'self-governments' in the outer islands in the 1920s[6] – no Indonesian ruler now had contact with the rest of the world other than through the Dutch.

There was indeed a tension between the urge to integrate and the urge to control. Earlier in the nineteenth century, the Indies government, like the Company before it, had ruled on the cheap: it relied on native rulers, and even where it ruled directly, on native instrumentality. It wanted an integrated realm. But it also wanted to avoid challenge from within as well as challenge from without. Its realm-building, generally a slow process, was always an irregular one. The 'short declaration' that, at the end of the Aceh war, was to displace the more elaborate contracts with many of the rulers, was a step towards regularisation, but not a revolution. 'Peace and order', the watchwords of Baud, Colonial Minister and Governor-General before 1848, remained significant for a small colonial power that was attempting a large task.

Furthermore, its priorities, again not unlike the Company's, remained economic. The Dutch endeavour, as Clifford Geertz put it, was from the economic point of view 'one long endeavour to bring Indonesia's crops into the modern world, but not her people'.[7] A policy of peace and order was designed to avoid trouble that a weak power could not face, and which might even risk the intervention of others. But it was also designed as a means of obtaining economic advantage. That was particularly evident under the cultivation system, when the Javanese aristocracy was closely involved with the attempts to secure produce for export. Their role was indeed to be the focus of much of the criticism of that system, made when the States-General was able to debate the Indies and private capitalists were increasingly critical of state monopoly. The most famous document in that discourse is *Max Havelaar*, a novel by Douwes Dekker (Multatuli). '[S]trangers came from the West... They wished to make profits of the productiveness of the soil and commanded the native to devote part of his labours and time to the growth of... products which would yield a greater

5

margin of gain in the *European* markets. To make the lower man do this, a very simple policy sufficed. He obeys his chiefs, and so it was only necessary to win over those chiefs by promising them part of the profit, and...the scheme succeeded completely.'[8]

The economic policies of the Dutch also transformed the relationship of the islands with the rest of the world. In earlier times there had been two main foci of economic activity. One was the entrepot traffic, available to political entities that had positional advantage, in particular where the trade of the islands linked up with the traffic to India and China. Sri Vijaya had enjoyed such a position. So, later, did Melaka, the first port to be captured by the Portuguese in 1511, only to be lost to the Dutch in 1641. The other focus of economic activity was east and central Java. By contrast with much of the rest of the archipelago, it was relatively fertile, and able to sustain a substantial rural population, and a dynastic system bearing some comparison with the feudal structures of western Europe. At Batavia the VOC was placing itself between these two foci of economic activity and political power. For two centuries it was also the focus of an Asia-wide economic endeavour. In the nineteenth century, it became the administrative capital of Netherlands India. It was also one of the ports through which the Dutch sought to channel the Indies' trade, which now was more and more a colonial one. No longer were the Dutch profiting from the intra-Asian trade. Their profit now came from securing coffee and sugar from Java, and, increasingly, selling there textiles from Twente and Overijssel.

The islands were connected with the world in ways other than the political and the economic, in particular through religion. Indeed earlier rulers and peoples would not have recognised such divisions among human activities. In the Buddhist or Hindu-Buddhist states of Sri Viyaja and Majapahit, the ruler had a special role and might even be an incarnation of a deity, and ritual surrounded him and underpinned the administration. The Islamisation of the islands, which increased in impetus with the founding of Melaka, also saw a transformation of its political structures, though not necessarily their complete elimination. The advent of the Europeans in some respects stimulated Islam and domesticated it. Reacting against the Portuguese capture of Melaka, new Muslim sultanates appeared, Aceh and Makasar among them. Islam identified with resistance to the Europeans, and a different link with the outer world was thus established. Much of the resistance to the Dutch in the colonial phase had an Islamic aspect to it, most famously, of course, that of Dipo Negoro in the 1820s, the Aceh war, too. Their reliance on the *adat* chiefs for peace and order could not but provoke a closer identification between the peasants and the Islamic leaders.

The opening of the Suez canal in 1869, though not of course so intended, intensified the links with the Islamic homeland. The political and economic links of the colonial period, particularly with the Netherlands, but also with other parts of the world, facilitated many other contacts as well. Within their territories, furthermore, the Dutch provided limited opportunities for Western education, initially for economic reasons, and later with a rather larger purpose. Improved communications within Netherlands India, as well as with the outside world, also contributed to a cultural ferment in which Indonesians, as some of them came to see themselves, felt both a greater sense of unity among themselves, and also a greater distinctiveness among peoples. Where the local Dutch, the Chinese communities, resident or 'sojourning', the Eurasians, fitted in, if at all, remained to be determined: to some extent the growing sense of Indonesian identification was predicated on their marginalisation or exclusion.

These changes contributed to the rise of an Indonesian nationalism. That was itself a process, the outcomes of which were not predetermined. But the process necessarily involved a growing sense of unity, at least among the elite, and a growing perception among them that such unity could and should be expressed in a sense of nationhood. The European world of nations with colonies and dependencies was to become a world of nations in the European style. The colonial leaders aspired to form nation-states in a world of nation-states. In some cases it helped to win them international support, even in the metropolis. At home it required the recruitment of mass support. There the leaders had to compete or work with the colonial government, the old elite which had often worked with it, the Islamic elite which generally had not. To inform the masses, still largely rural, of the concept of nation and state was a tough task. Often the masses saw the struggle differently, as one against an alien government, against the infidel, against the dislocation of old ways of life by economic, administrative, and social change.

The colonial power was, partly wittingly, partly unwittingly, building a political entity in Netherlands India that was changing its relationship with the rest of the world. In the early twentieth century, some of its leaders, the Ethici, saw that the relationship with the Netherlands would have to change. They tended to stop short of advocating independence, but preferred to believe in some form of association with the 'motherland'. Indeed Ethical Policy was a means to defend the Indies. Pointing to the fate of Spain in the Philippines, van Deventer suggested in 1899 that 'there is no better way of ensuring that we keep the East Indies than a policy of righteousness and honesty'.[9] The new elite could be brought to recognise the continued value of an association with the Netherlands if it were put on a new basis. But that basis was not the relationship of one independent state with another. Increasingly these views were shaped by the emergence of the nationalist movement. In face of it some of the Dutch became more conservative and were inclined to revert to 'peace and order' policies, or to insist on the validity of *adat*, or custom, and to emphasise the diversity of the Indies.

The nationalist movement also offered a recipe for the emergence of a modern state. In some sense its view was shaped by the policies of the colonial state itself, the two movements indeed reacting against each other and working in combination. It faced the opposition of the 'police state', state control over education, limits on participation. It fought against divide-and-rule by insisting on unity. 'It is the responsibility of each and every one of us to study these three aspects', nationalism, Islam, and Marxism, Sukarno argued, 'and to show that these three "waves" can work together to form a single, gigantic and irresistible tidal wave.' He was 'convinced that it is only this unity which will bring us to the realization of our dreams: a Free Indonesia'.[10] Generally without weapons, the nationalist movement endeavoured to evoke popular support, often working against, sometimes co-opting collaborationist leaders, utilising ideologies not squarely nationalist, enlisting religious impulses sometimes xenophobic in approach rather than inclusive. With a vision of the future as a nation among nations and a state among states, it also recognised the importance of support from nations and states, emerging and actual, outside the colonial framework.

The emergence of Communism was both advantage and disadvantage. It assisted nationalists and it hindered them. It gave them an additional organisational capacity and an additional appeal, but its aims were not co-terminous with theirs. Tensions were apparent almost from the start, within the proto-nationalist Islamic League (Sarekat Islam) as it became a mass movement, within nationalist movements that were concerned lest social disruption undermine political ambition. Nor did the Communists always escape the millenarian thrust that Marx both felt and sought to contain: in Indonesian society, indeed, the millenarian traditions were a reason for the popularity of Communism. They also undermined its long-term success. Communist uprisings were premature. And they intensified reaction on the part of the colonial ruler. Indeed the link between Communism and nationalism was counterproductive in this respect as well. The violence and extremism were arguments for overall repression, and for the abandonment of the Ethical Policy, for the recrudescence of *adat*-based policies, for Governor-General De Jonge. 'A world-wide conspiracy of international communism was detected in the most improbable organizations', especially after the insurrections of 1926–7.[11]

Nor was Communism an unequivocal advantage in the shaping of Netherlands India's changing relationship with the world. Nationalist movements could look to the example of other nations, to the success of the Japanese, to the Chinese revolution of 1911, to *swaraj* and non-cooperation in British India, to Kemal Ataturk. Communist movements, too, could look for inspiration overseas: the movement was, after all, based on an allegedly universal concept; and the creators of the Soviet state were 'internationalists'. But their aim was not a world of nations. At most their nationalism was a strategy rather than an objective in itself. Nationalists were, therefore, always at a tangent with Communists internationally as they were internally. Each might find a use for the other, but their marriages were marriages of convenience. And sometimes of inconvenience. For, while Communists might precipitate crisis with the colonial power by premature action, by 'adventurism', so also, too, their relationship with a foreign power of universalist pretensions gave nationalists a problem and colonial rulers an argument. Could nationalists use the Communists and yet retain their purpose? Was nationalism pushed or deflected by a foreign power or a foreign influence?

In the event the colonial regime was displaced not by internal opposition, nor by Communist subversion, but by the Japanese invasion of 1942. That affected all the terms in the equation. Economically the Japanese broke off the links with the European and American economies. Culturally, they boosted the role of Islam, played down the role of Dutch, encouraged the use of Indonesian, attempted to develop a youth culture, promoted a Japan-led movement of Asia for the Asiatics. Politically they destroyed the colonial power and gave its adversaries, the nationalists, new opportunities, in administration, in the army, even in politics, though, of course, severing their Communist connexions. At the same time, Japan treated the frontiers of Netherlands India arbitrarily, and it had no real interest in promoting independence till what turned out to be the last year of the war.[12]

The defeat of the Japanese in 1945 was followed by an attempt to restore the colonial regime. By that time the Indonesians led by Sukarno and Hatta had on 17 August proclaimed a Republic, and the Dutch were never able to reach what they saw as a satisfactory accommodation with it. 'And why must Indonesia willy-nilly be made partner of a commonwealth in which the Dutch tail will wag the Indonesian dog?' Hatta asked. 'The Dutch are graciously permitting us entry into the basement while we have climbed all the way to the top floor and up to the attic.'[13] They believed that there were more moderate elements in Indonesia whose collaboration they could evoke on a more-or-less prewar model, backing that collaborative system as in colonial times with a limited use of force. But their attempts to re-introduce this pattern failed, and their resort to force in two police actions in 1947 and 1948 in fact made the republic stronger. At the same time the international position changed, and the republican leadership was adept at taking advantage of it. It welcomed the mediation of the British, anxious to withdraw their largely Indian troops, yet still hoping for reconciliation between the Europeans and the Indonesians. The republic welcomed support from India and Australia, and from the United Nations, to which those states took its case. Above all, the republicans won the support of the US, in particular by putting down the Communists, who initiated another ill-timed revolt at Madiun in September 1948. The Indonesians secured independence, partly by their continued guerilla struggle within Indonesia, partly by their diplomatic struggle outside Indonesia. They neatly reversed the colonial recipe of force and collaboration with guerilla struggle and internationalisation.

The republic had been proclaimed in 1945. The independence of the Republic of the United States of Indonesia was acknowledged in 1949. It was recognised by other states and took its seat in the UN, the two signs of independent statehood in the postwar world. Emerging from a struggle with a colonial power that had limited democracy, winning support from the leading democratic power after a war fought against non-democratic powers, the new state endorsed democracy. Though it had the trappings of a democratic state – parties, parliament, cabinet – it did not hold elections till 1955. Then there was a massive and impressive turn-out. Yet in some ways the elections may have destroyed the democratic experiment. The struggle against the Dutch had tended to muffle the divisions among Indonesians which the colonial power had liked to emphasise. The end of the struggle revealed deep differences about the next step: what kind of Indonesia should an independent Indonesia be? The federal structure, tarred with the Dutch brush, was quickly abandoned. But that focused the divisions on the central government in Jakarta, as Batavia had now become. The governmental instability that ensued would, it was thought, be ended by the elections. They indeed produced a decisive result. But it tended to polarise the interests of Java and the outer islands, and within less than a year a series of regional revolts ensued. Martial law was established, and the power of the army, inheriting, too, the prestige of the guerilla struggle, was increased.

For a while President Sukarno sought to sustain what he called 'guided democracy'. Indonesia would not abandon democracy, but pursue its own consensual version. But many of the parties had been undermined by the elections, or discredited by association with the regional revolts, and in a sense there was no democracy left to guide. Instead of eliciting consensus, the President was reduced to a precarious balancing act between the army and the Communist Party, which had revived since the Madiun disaster by pursuing a nationalist and populist but not revolutionary line. In 1965, it seems that premature action once more led the communists to disaster. Though its origins remain controversial, the attempted Gestapu coup of 1 October precipitated a seizure of power by the army, now led by Suharto, commander of the Army Strategic Reserve (KOSTRAD). Under the *dwifungsi* concept, the army has never relinquished this power.

It is not perhaps facile to suggest a comparison between the colonial regime and the New Order. In both democratic politics is strictly limited. The letter is in part there, the spirit is not. The priority, it might be said, was once more peace and order. If the Dutch regime was dedicated to export, the New Order was dedicated to development. The Dutch regime had one advantage: there was a regular means for changing the ruler. By contrast, the stability of the Suharto era is always threatened by its very nature: it buys stability at a cost of uncertainty. How will the president be replaced? Who will succeed him? Will it happen peacefully?   ●

1   Cf J. D. Legge, *Sukarno: A Political Biography*, London: Penguin, 1972, p. 185.
2   C. R. Boxer, *Four Centuries of Portuguese Expansion*, Johannesburg: Witwatersrand University Press, 1965, p. 1.
3   A. van der Kraan, *Bali at War*, Melbourne: Monash University Press, 1995, p. 183.
4   C. Fasseur, *The Politics of Colonial Exploitation*, Ithaca, NY: Cornell University, Southeast Asia Program, 1992, p. 15.
5   G. J. Resink, *Indonesia's History between the Myths*, The Hague: van Hoeve, 1968, p. 238.
6   W. Middendorp, 'The Administration of the Outer Provinces of the Netherlands Indies', in B. Schrieke, ed., *The Effect of Western Influence on native civilisations in the Malay archipelago*, Batavia: Kolff, 1929, pp. 66–7.
7   C. Geertz, *Agricultural Involution*, Berkeley and Los Angeles: University of California Press, 1963, p. 48.
8   Multatuli, *Max Havelaar*, trans. W. Siebenhaar, Kuala Lumpur: Southdene, reprint 1984, p. 39.
9   quoted M. Kuitenbrouwer, *The Netherlands and the Rise of Modern Imperialism*, Oxford, NY: Berg, 1991, p. 258.
10 Sukarno, *Nationalism, Islam & Marxism*, trans, Ithaca, NY: Cornell University Press, 1970, p. 36.
11 Harry A. Poeze, 'Political Intelligence in the Netherlands Indies', in R. Cribb, ed., *The late colonial state in Indonesia*, Leiden: KITLV Press, 1994, pp. 239–41.
12 Ken'ichi Goto, 'Caught in the Middle: Japanese Attitudes towards Indonesian Independence in 1945', *Journal of Southeast Asian Studies*, 27, 1 (March 1990), p. 39.
13 quoted M. Rose, *Indonesia Free*, Ithaca, NY: Cornell University, Southeast Asia Program, 1987, p. 128.

MALAYSIA, SINGAPORE, BRUNEI

Malaya, like Indonesia, has a long history: but, for the most part, it is not the history of Malaya, and for even shorter time is it the history of Malaysia. Much of its history it indeed shares with the states that became Indonesia, some with states that are now part of Thailand. Again, it is only as a result of a number of interlinked processes that Malaysia has become a nation-state in the present world of nation-states. Those processes include the political action or inaction of the European powers, in this case in particular Britain; the economic changes brought to the region in the nineteenth and early twentieth centuries; religious, cultural and demographic developments; the emergence of nationalism; the Japanese interregnum; the cold war and decolonisation. They were changes the Malay Peninsula shared with the Indonesian archipelago, but the outcomes were different.

The peninsula, thinly-populated, was home to a number of Malay states, essentially river-mouth communities, some of which enjoyed a positional advantage that gave them a pre-eminence, but none of which imposed a political unity on the peninsula. In early times it seems that the states established on the narrow neck of the peninsula – in the region of Kra – were better placed than those to the south, able to benefit not only from local but from international commerce. Later, the route round the tip of the straits became more practicable, and major economic and political centres were established there. One of these, Temasek, which occupied the site of the present state of Singapore, appears to have been an outpost of a state in the archipelago, Sri Vijaya, for at least part of its history. The state of Melaka, which emerged in the fourteenth and early fifteenth centuries CE, and identified its cause with Islam, again owed its success to its ability to turn its positional advantages to account. It was a successor to Sri Vijaya. That demonstrates again that peninsula and archipelago shared their history. The straits, now so important to the international connexions of the region, were also a link within the region.

Pursuing a share of the trade within Asia, and particularly in spices, including clove and nutmeg then produced mainly in Maluku, the Portuguese struck at the entrepot of Melaka in 1511. For its capture the great Affonso de Albuquerque adduced two arguments: 'the great service which we shall perform to Our Lord in casting the Moors out of this country'; and 'the additional service which we shall render to the King D.

Manuel in taking this city, because it is the headquarters of all the spiceries and drugs which the Moors carry every year hence to the Straits without our being able to prevent them from so doing'.[1] The Portuguese were not, however, otherwise interested in the peninsula, and there, as in the archipelago, their effect was not to monopolise power but to disperse it. One great sultanate was destroyed. But its leaders moved south to found another, based at Johor-Lingga-Riau at the tip of the straits. The Portuguese venture, provoking religious as well as economic and political opposition, also prompted the creation of other rivals, in particular Aceh, a Muslim state based in north Sumatra, but keenly interested in the peninsula as well. The straits were now no more a dividing line than they had been before. Indeed the states contested the control of the straits, at times in alliance with and at times in opposition to the Portuguese, a new element in the politics of the area, but not builders of a state in peninsula or archipelago.

The Dutch did not immediately displace the Portuguese in Melaka: their centre was Batavia. But as their determination to control the trade of the archipelago was intensified by the onset of the seventeenth-century recession, they took further steps against the Portuguese and against the independent sultanates. In some cases they secured the help of the latter against the former, though the results could ultimately only be unfortunate for both. Nevertheless the Dutch capture of Melaka in 1641 led to a period of prosperity for Johor, marred only at the end of the century by an internecine dispute, the overthrow of the old dynasty, and the incursions of Bugis adventurers from Sulawesi, dislodged by the Dutch and Arung Palakka, the ruler of Bone, of whose life Leonard Andaya has written a brilliant account.[2] Johor retained a prestige derived from its past history, but it did not exert control over other states on the peninsula. One of those that prospered for a time was Pattani, now part of Thailand.

Though the control of the Dutch was limited, their presence tended to restrict the advance of the Thais into the peninsula, an objective Melaka had sought by opening contacts with the Chinese. But the Dutch established only commercial and contractual connexions with the peninsular states, concentrating in particular on the tin-bearing state of Perak, and even there Aceh contested their monopoly. In the eighteenth century, as the range of their power diminished, the Dutch saw Melaka more as an outpost of Java than as an asset in itself. They became increasingly concerned by the activities of the British, now on their way to becoming the leading European power. They were penetrating into areas where Dutch control was limited and Dutch treaties could be challenged, and making contacts with the Bugis, particularly at Riau. Over that the Dutch asserted control in 1784 through a treaty with Johor.

The incursion of the British into the region was less for its own sake than for the sake of their other interests. Those included the security of their growing empire in India and of their expanding tea trade with China. Those interests indeed gave them interests in the peninsula and archipelago, but their priorities were elsewhere. Moreover, they were anxious for a positive relationship with the Dutch in Europe. There, as elsewhere, the French were now their rivals, and it was important to deny the French the opportunity to dominate the Dutch Republic and thus, too, its holdings overseas. The British sought to realise their objectives in Southeast Asia without alienating the Dutch. In 1786 they acquired Penang from the sultan of Kedah, who was anxious for help against the Thais. It was on the periphery of Dutch interests, but it might afford some security for the British in the Bay of Bengal. They hesitated to move south, where Riau might be a useful entrepot for archipelagic produce that would supplement the trade to China, and they failed to secure it in the Anglo-Dutch negotiations of the 1780s.

The situation was changed by the wars that followed the French revolution of 1789, but not completely transformed. If the Dutch Republic was now dominated by the French, or by pro-French groups, it was important for the British to pre-empt them in the Indies. In 1795–6 Melaka was taken, and also Maluku. After peace was made at Amiens in 1801, they were returned, though that had not happened in the case of Melaka by the time the war recommenced. Only in the course of the renewed war did the British, recapturing Maluku, also proceed against Java in 1811. When peace returned the Dutch possessions were restored, and the idea of a British empire in the islands, put up by Stamford Raffles, disapproved. He secured, however, instructions which he used to found a settlement at Singapore in 1819 – on 'classic ground', as he saw it[3] – and regaining Melaka once more, and continuing to hold Penang, the British East India Company became the possessor of what were called the Straits Settlements. As the name suggests, it was not a Malayan state. The settlements looked outward, rather than inward.

During the subsequent decades, however, the settlements, largely on local initiative, developed connexions with the peninsular states, particularly Kedah and Johor. One object was to limit the advance of the Thais, who not only controlled Pattani but claimed Kedah as a vassal. Another aim was to suppress piracy, and more generally to bring order to the peninsula. Malay rulers responded, particular Ibrahim, the ruler of Johor, who lived in Singapore, and Sultan Omar of Trengganu, apprehensive of the Thais, but also of aggrandisement on the part of Johor.

In the 1870s the British government, now working through the Colonial Office itself rather than the East India Company, authorised intervention in states on the west coast. Again it was a pragmatic and limited policy. These states, particularly Perak and Selangor, were the scene of tin-mining initiatives and substantial Chinese immigration, and the resulting imbalance of power and civil struggle prompted calls for intervention. There was also a fear that another European state might intervene if Britain did not, and, while the peninsula was itself still of limited significance, the straits, the road to China, still had to be kept free of a major power. The intervention was, however, shaped by what seemed to be the lessons of Britain's connexion with Malay states so far. It was a matter of advice and guidance. Treaties were made, installing Residents whose advice, except in matters of religion and custom, had to be sought and acted upon. Not that it was in practice a simple matter. Hugh Low was sent to Perak. 'When I asked Mr Meade [at the Colonial Office] "who was the rajah I was sent to advise?" He said, "We don't know of one, you must try to ascertain whether there is any one fit for the position, and then he will be supported".'[4]

Subsequently this system was extended to the state of Pahang, and the Federated Malay States (FMS) was set up as a result of additional treaties in 1895. That was perhaps part, too, of a more general trend in British imperial policy towards federation, not, as was often publicly suggested, in terms of imperial federation, but in terms of strengthening individual parts of the empire. The empire had long been highly decentralised, and self-government in the settler colonies had confirmed that trend. The only practical way in which the empire might be made stronger in a changing world – where the emerging super-powers were the US and Russia – was by making its constituent parts stronger and relying on their acting in fact as allies rather than as superordinates and subordinates. The process took place first with what came to be called Dominions. But it applied in other territories yet far from that status. Creating the FMS was not just the result of a desire for efficiency or development: it was part of an imperial change.

It did not, however, yet amount to creating a united state. The Straits Settlements was a colony; the federated states were not British territory at all. There remained, too, Malay states outside the federation, including Johor, which enjoyed a privileged position because of a long-established informal connexion with the British, and the northern states, Kedah, Perlis, Kelantan and Trengganu. The local British authorities had endeavoured to prevent these states falling under Thai dominance. They had failed in one sense – the British government had come to recognise Thai claims in the 1860s and 1870s – but succeeded in another – they limited the effective implementation of those claims. Sir Frank Swettenham was among those who sought to bring these states into a formal relationship with the British, and Siam finally transferred its claims in 1909 as part of a wider Anglo-Thai deal.

Even though Swettenham wrote of 'British Malaya',[5] the transfer still did not create a unified Malay state on the peninsula. There were still three groups of territories: Straits Settlements, Federated Malay States, and Unfederated Malay States. The northern sultans were not keen to accept British officials, and the centralisation that marked the development of the

FMS made the prospective loss of power additionally uninviting. The officers appointed in the end were indeed called 'advisers' and not 'Residents'. Partly because of that, and partly because the states did not fully share in the economic and demographic changes of the west coast states, quite different styles of administration developed, quite different approaches to the Malay community.

The urge to a greater degree of unification was, not altogether paradoxically, accompanied by a programme of decentralisation: if the states within the FMS had greater powers, other states might be more ready to join. 'Until the knot now tied so tightly in the Federated States can be loosened', wrote Sir Samuel Wilson of the Colonial Office, after visiting Malaya in 1932, 'it would appear hopeless to suggest that the Rulers of the Unfederated States should come into any form of Malayan League, or even agree to meet together periodically to discuss matters of common interest.'[6] Decentralisation, a theme of British political endeavours in Malaya in the 1920s and the 1930s, made little progress for a number of reasons. One was resistance within the FMS. Would a looser federation be so effective a guarantee of development? Would Kuala Lumpur, the FMS capital, be subordinated to Singapore? After the frustrations of the 1920s, Sir Cecil Clementi attempted a bold initiative as Governor and High Commissioner in the early 1930s. His very boldness, however, perhaps made substantial change even less likely: it brought out the opposition. And amid all the insecurities of the 1930s, the British had no wish to provoke intractable problems on the peninsula, the resources of which, with the development of rubber, had become so important a dollar-earner for the sterling area.

Economically, indeed, the peninsula had been increasingly drawn into a relationship with the rest of the world. In earlier centuries the resources of the peninsula, in particular the tin of Perak and the marine produce of the Johor archipelago, had been important to the trade with China, but the entrepot activities of Melaka and Riau had been perhaps of even greater significance. In the nineteenth century, the situation, initially at least, changed quantitatively rather than qualitatively. The main British interest was in the new entrepot trade of Singapore, and then in the tin deposits of Perak and Selangor. Only after the turn of the century – with the development of the motor car, and the initiative of H. N. Ridley in introducing *Hevea brasiliensis* – did the peninsula become in itself of major economic value to the British: it became a leading rubber producer and thus a leading dollar-earner. That, of course, gave Singapore another dimension, too, though it retained its distinctive interest in the entrepot trade of the region.

Culturally the settlements, in particular Singapore, played an important role on the peninsula. They were, of course, sources for the spread of European culture in the nineteenth century, with the mission at Melaka, and the Keasberry school at Singapore, as well as being the base for the highest

British official, the Governor/High Commissioner. The settlements were also the avenue of other changes. They were both recipients of Chinese immigration, and also transit points for the Chinese and the Indians who worked in tin mines and on rubber plantations. Finally they linked Muslim Malaya with reformist or 'shari'ah-minded' Islam.[7]

In Indonesia and in other countries in the region, nationalism helped to shape the emergence of new states, though normally within the frontiers the colonial powers had established or were establishing. In Malaya its role was more equivocal, for there were nationalisms rather than nationalism, and the Malays were ceasing to be a majority. Though the immigrant communities were in fact becoming more settled in Malaya, and increasing numbers of Chinese and Indians were born there, their political interest tended to be in Congress or in the struggles of the KMT (Kuomintang) and the Chinese Communist Party, and national leaders from India and China sought their support. The national consciousness of the Malay community was, on the other hand, overwhelmingly affected by the substantial presence of the immigrant communities, in particular the Chinese. Malays tended to emphasise the extent to which the immigrants remained immigrants, the sojourners sojourners, and tended themselves to stress allegiance to their rulers and to the British protectors. The more extreme among them, on the other hand, began to think in terms of an identification with Indonesian nationalism. In a Greater Indonesia Malays might find a support against the Chinese that did not identify them with the rulers and the imperialists.

Though the Japanese dislodged the colonial power, as in Indonesia, in Malaya they did less to promote nationalism. Indeed they damaged what territorial integrity it had by transferring the northern states back to Thailand, while administering the peninsula in connection with Sumatra. Moreover, they handled each community differently. The Chinese were the main butt of their policies, though some prospered in the chaotic conditions they created. Elements of the Indian community were given a new sense of purpose by the creation of the Indian National Army. Malays were given a greater political and administrative role, and while the Japanese did not hold out the prospect of independence, some made links with the Indonesians.

The British returned after the war, though they did not have to reconquer, as they had expected. Indeed there was an interregnum, during which there were unprecedented clashes between the Malay and Chinese communities: 'the conflict in Johore ... assumed all the characteristics of a race war'.[8] British wartime planning was dedicated to building a Malayan Union, with a central government at Kuala Lumpur and a much more limited role for the states. The British also planned to identify immigrants with the union by creating a new form of citizenship, diminishing the appeal that China, a wartime ally, was expected to exert. Implementing this plan proved impossible. The Malays, politicised by the war and by the interregnum, bitterly opposed the union and boycotted the installation of its governor, Sir Edward Gent, in April 1946. That, however, had the effect of identifying Malay nationalism with the rulers, thus giving it a special cast. Apprehensive of the appeal of Indonesian nationalism, the British accepted the outcome. A federal solution after all gave them the unified Malaya they had sought since the 1920s. But the Chinese community felt betrayed, and that contributed to the Communist revolt, or 'Emergency', of 1948.

Paradoxically it was this that did most to prompt a new kind of nation-building. The British recognised that the emergency could not be ended by force alone, and that it was essential to encourage an alternative Chinese leadership. At the same time, Malay leaders recognised that a deal with the Chinese community was necessary if Malaya were to attain its independence sooner rather than later. Most believed that even these political developments would require many years of endeavour. In fact the United Malays National Organisation (UMNO) and the Malayan Chinese Association (MCA) collaborated in the Kuala Lumpur elections of 1952, and it was the practice of intercommunal electoral collaboration that enabled Malaya to win its independence in 1957.[9] The bargain was based on Malay political leadership and Chinese economic opportunity.

The crisis for this deal came in 1969. The riots of that year indicated popular Malay discontent with it, and a New Economic Policy was implemented, designed to transfer a share of the economy to the Malays. A powerful Malay middle class was created and the earlier balance changed. The economic expansion of the 1980s and 1990s reduced the tensions this might have engendered, and the Prime Minister, Dr Mahathir, sought to focus attention on an extraordinarily ambitious programme to transform Malaysia into a modern industrialised state by 2020.

Malaysia had been created in 1963 by uniting the federation, Singapore, Sarawak and Sabah (North Borneo). Singapore had been kept out of the union when it was created and was kept out of the federation that replaced it. That was partly justified by its strategic importance for Britain in the region as a whole. It also had long-standing entrepot interests that arguably required it to be handled separately. Perhaps the conclusive reason was its predominantly Chinese population. Including Singapore would turn the balance against the Malays in a unified state, and make union yet more difficult to implement. It was still envisaged that the political development of peninsula and island would, however, converge. Indeed the People's Action Party (PAP), which came to power in Singapore shortly after Malaya became independent, believed that union was necessary for economic survival. The conclusion it drew from the war was that 'no one – neither the Japanese nor the British – had the right to push and kick us around. We are determined that we could govern ourselves and bring up our children in a country where we can be proud to be self-respecting people.'[10] The PAP's hope was of independence through 'merger'. Where else could a market for an industrialised Singapore be found? How could a socialist economy be built otherwise?

Singapore was thus ready to join Malaysia for economic reasons when it was proposed by the UMNO leader, Tunku Abdul Rahman, in 1961. From the Malayan point of view, it was also seen as a means of countering the apparently leftward trend of Singapore politics. The inclusion of so many additional Chinese was to be made acceptable by also including the Borneo territories, thus permitting their decolonisation.

In retrospect this seems an extraordinarily ambitious undertaking in state-building. The British had contemplated some bringing together of the territories since the 1890s; it had been in Clementi's capacious mind, too; and wartime planners had talked of a Union of Southeast Asia and established a Governor-General. Now it was an exercise in decolonisation, not without comparison in the West Indies and Central Africa. It survived in part. Singapore left in 1965, but Sarawak and Sabah remain a part of the larger federation.

David Marshall, the Chief Minister, had denied Singapore was 'too small to become an independent state'. It had a larger population and a larger revenue than six current UN members, Costa Rica, Iceland, Jordan, Libya, Nicaragua, and Panama.[11] The British had thought by contrast that it was not big enough to survive independently, and the PAP itself had seen a merger as a guarantee of economic and political survival. The new republic in the event more than survived: it flourished. A determined government made brilliant use of the economic opportunities provided by Japanese and US investment, and then sought with some success to ensure that this would be not merely a temporary utilisation of cheap labour, but the foundation for further development. At the same time, it generally endeavoured to avoid alienating its neighbours, an island of Chinese in a Malay world as it was.

Sarawak and Sabah were states set up by the British in the nineteenth century in a somewhat haphazard series of initiatives. The first step towards a Sarawak state was taken by James Brooke, who was to become the first of its so-called white rajas in 1841. He believed that the Dutch should not predominate throughout the archipelago, and initially hoped to counter them by reforming the sultanate of Brunei, of which Sarawak was then part. In fact he and his successor, Charles, ended by creating a more or less independent Sarawak state at Brunei's expense, and by 1890 its frontiers had reached the Limbang itself. Much of the territory of the British North Borneo Company, chartered in 1881, was also granted by Brunei, though some also by the neighbouring island sultanate of Sulu. The Raj of Sarawak and the state of North Borneo, like the remnant of Brunei itself, became British protectorates in 1888. 'It would seem that the prospect of a uniform British policy in the Malay Indies, including Borneo as well as the Malay

Peninsula, will most be furthered in future years, as communications both by land and sea become quicker and more constant, by entrusting the governor at the central point of Singapore with powers of general supervision and control.'[12] This was the view of C. P. Lucas, one of the proponents of the FMS, but no Borneo federation was set up. After the Second World War, Sarawak and North Borneo (Sabah) belatedly became British colonies as part of Britain's planned reconstruction of Southeast Asia, but still no federation followed, even among them. In the event, the territories were to join Malaysia and the opposition thus aroused, particularly from Indonesian 'Confrontation', helped to consolidate, rather than dislocate, the connexion.

Brunei, in which the British had placed a Resident in 1906, stayed out. Though now small, and indeed in two parts unconnected by land, it had become very wealthy as a result of the discovery and exploitation of its oil and gas. Finding a place in the new Malaysia would have meant losing control of that wealth. It would also have submerged a proud dynasty. Nor could the British push the Bruneis. 'We have proclaimed to the world that no pressure has been and, by implication will be, put on the people of Brunei to join Malaysia. For us to go back on that now could hardly fail to undermine all confidence in British good faith; and nowhere would the effects be more apparent than in Indonesia.'[13] Finally abandoning British protection in 1984, Brunei became the only independent Malay monarchy in the world. 'We are a new nation, but an ancient country', Sultan Hassanal Bolkiah told the UN: one of Asia's oldest. '. . . So we have known pride and glory. But we have also experienced much pain.'[14]   ●

---

1   quoted *The Commentaries of the Great Afonso Dalboquerque*, trans W. de G. Birch, London: Hakluyt Society, 1875–84, III, pp. 116–18.

2   Leonard Y. Andaya, *The Heritage of Arung Palakka*, The Hague: Nijhoff, 1987.

3   quoted C. M. Turnbull, *A History of Singapore*, Kuala Lumpur: Oxford University Press, 1977, p. 1.

4   Low/Robinson, 28/5/1878. CO882/4, Public Record Office, London.

5   F. A. Swettenham, *British Malaya*, London: Lane, 1907.

6   *Report...on his visit...*, *Great Britain Parliamentary Papers*, Cmd 4276, p. 12.

7   A. Milner, *The Invention of Politics in Colonial Malaya*, Cambridge: Cambridge University Press, 1995, p. 156.

8   Halinah Bamadhaj, 'The Impact of the Japanese Occupation of Malaya on Malay Society and Politics (1941–1945)', MA thesis, University of Auckland, 1975, p. 197.

9   Cf Irene Tinker, 'Malayan Elections: electoral pattern for plural societies?', *Western Political Quarterly*, IX (1956), pp. 258–82.

10   quoted Ernest Chew and Edwin Lee, eds, *A History of Singapore*, Singapore: Oxford University Press, 1991, p. 117.

11 Memorandum, April 1956. Singapore Constitutional Conference, *Great Britain Parliamentary Papers*, Cmd. 9777, Appendix 4.
12 Memorandum in SofS/Governor, 19/5/1893, quoted P. L. Burns, 'The constitutional history of Malaya', PhD thesis, University of London, 1966, p. 230.
13 quoted B. A. Hussainmiya, *Sultan Omar Ali Saiffudin III and Britain*, Kuala Lumpur/Oxford: Oxford University Press, 1995, p. 316.
14 quoted Lord Chalfont, *By God's Will*, London: Weidenfeld, 1989, p. 179.

THE PHILIPPINES

The opposition to the creation of Malaysia did not come only from Indonesia; it came also from the Philippines. Sulu was part of its territory, and it put in a claim to Sabah, on the ground that the British had leased it from the sultan. That claim the Filipinos had not seen fit to make when the British had transformed the status of North Borneo (Sabah) in 1946, but they recognised that the inclusion of the territory in the new Malaysian state would destroy their hopes completely. A post-colonial state might hope to inherit a colony, but not the territory of another nation. The claim had, moreover, been associated with earlier manifestations of Philippines nationalism and with the Filipino aspiration to play a distinctive leadership role in the Malay world. In 1922 Representative Villanueva had argued that 'the acquisition of Borneo would be a step towards the formation of a greater Philippines, and would bring the day nearer when the proposed Pan-Malayan association of federated peoples would be realised'.[1]

Though the Philippines had an uncertain southern frontier, in other respects it was more integrated than either Indonesia or Malaya/Malaysia. That was largely the result of colonial endeavour, which certainly played a larger role in the history of the Philippines than it did in the history of Indonesia, partly because the previous history of the two island groups was so different. The Philippines lay rather apart from the main trade routes that had connected the Malay peninsula and the Indonesian archipelago with India, and along which Hinduism, Buddhism and Islam had travelled. What it produced was not in demand elsewhere; it was not especially fertile; and though it had connexions with China and with eastern parts of the Indonesian archipelago, it contained no wide-ranging commercial entrepot. In the late fifteenth century, the chief state was in the south, the sultanate of Sulu. Though the sultanate of Brunei, 'a trading empire based on control of the sea',[2] was expanding trade and contact even as far north as Manila, most of the archipelago was in the hands of non-state entities, *barangay* or supra-*barangay* structures. Only one of the world's great religions, Islam, had taken hold and, again, mainly in the south.

The impact of the Spaniards was as a result all the more dramatic. To the south they contended violently but largely ineffectually with the Moro sultanates. They curbed the influence of Brunei, but they failed to destroy Sulu, and indeed commenced an endless struggle of raiding and counter-raiding within the islands they saw fit to name after the future King Philip II. But north of Mindanao and Sulu, they established their hold on the *barangays* both by co-opting the elites and by supporting the missionary Catholicism of the Franciscans, Dominicans, and Jesuits. The Philippines was drawn into a political unity earlier than the Indonesian archipelago and the peninsula, at least so far as Luzon and the Visayas were concerned. Much of their population was furthermore converted to Christianity, making it quite distinct from the rest of Southeast Asia in another respect as well.

In the nineteenth century the Spaniards continued their self-allocated role as state-builders. One task was to round out their realm. That included, on the one hand, attempts to secure control over the interior of Luzon. For the most part their control had so far tended to be coastal. Mountainous areas were not under it, and remontados escaped the elite, the friars, and the constabulary. Trade took place across internal frontiers. Nineteenth-century governors extended the control of the government, often in military forms. From the 1840s and 1850s, politico-military administrations were being established in the mountain regions of northern Luzon.[3] The Spaniards also tackled a yet tougher task, bringing the Moro lands under control. That was never fully achieved. The introduction of steamers helped to rid the islands of piracy. Military expeditions brought control over Mindanao. But after several attempts, only footholds were established in Sulu, and the sultan was still in a position to make a separate treaty with the US after it displaced Spain. 'At night, at frequent intervals, was heard the sharp cry of Alerte passing from one water tower to another along the city wall', Ada Pryer had written on a visit from Sandakan in 1898. 'It seems that the Spaniards are in constant fear that their town may be rushed by the Sulus and the greatest precautions are taken to avoid anything of the sort.'[4]

The Philippines were again set apart from the rest of the Malay world by the American conquest, an outcome of the Spanish-American war of 1898. That placed the islands in the hands of a major power. Though it was ambiguous about its imperial role, the US did not accept the republic that had been constituted at Malolos. Nor was it accepted by other states: the Philippines was not to go the way the trans-Pacific possessions of the Spaniards had gone earlier in the century. There were no independent states in Asia to take up its cause, as India was to take up Indonesia's in the 1940s. Only the Japanese, who had recently occupied neighbouring Taiwan, offered some demi-official support: General Kawakami of the Army General Staff 'doubted that the business would succeed, but felt that for the long-term interests of fifty or even one hundred years it was essential for Japan to have a friendly and grateful group of admirers in the Philippines'.[5] The fate of Korea does not suggest that their intervention would have advanced the cause of Philippines independence. US intervention deterred the Germans, as it deterred the Japanese. Much of the Filipino elite was won over, while military force was deployed in Luzon, and of course in Mindanao and Sulu. There, indeed, the conflict was more extended: only with Pershing's attack on Bagsak in 1913 was resistance ended.[6]

Fear of internal subversion and apprehension of other powers were not the only arguments that affected the elite: the US expected the Filipinos to take part in the government of the Philippines, and envisaged independence at some as yet unspecified date. That prospect prompted the Filipinos to struggle for independence. In so doing, however, they were also building on the experiences of the Spanish period. Then indeed they had been able to challenge their colonial rulers and almost to break them. A republic had been proclaimed in 1896, and the colonial rulers had bought a truce in 1897.

The Spaniards had, albeit unintentionally, made a major contribution to this movement: they had created some of the conditions for it, and then they had frustrated it, a fatal combination. Their rule had been in part based on the missionaries, and they had been more generous with educational opportunities than the Dutch. They had been less able than the Dutch to turn the power of government to economic advantage. While the nineteenth century had witnessed a striking development of export agriculture in the Philippines, it had largely been the work of foreign capital and local enterprise, in Central Luzon, where rice had been grown for export, in the Bikol region, the source of hemp, in the Visayas, which became a major source of sugar. The '*brutes*' grew rich, and their sons were educated. But the regime did not respond to the social and political aspirations these changes nurtured, despite, for example, the recommendations of Sinibaldo de Mas. He had advocated reforms, but did not believe they would be implemented; 'and the Philippines will become emancipated violently with great loss to properties and lives of Europeans and Filipino Spaniards. I think it would be infinitely much easier, more useful and more glorious for us to achieve the merit of the work, by forestalling it with generosity.'[7] No such policy was followed. The graduates of Santo Tomas, for example, could not secure the official posts for which they were fitted, as a memorial of 1887 pointed out.[8] Initially the new elite was extraordinarily moderate, but the repression on the part of the Spaniards drove it towards revolution, reluctant as leaders like José Rizal were. Following the 'Propaganda' movement of the 1880s, he founded the Liga Filipina in 1892, designed to confront the colonial regime with unity among its subjects: he feared the effects of violence.

Thus by the late nineteenth century, the Philippines was, unlike Malaya and Indonesia, a territory in which the members of the elite were beginning to think of themselves in national terms. Their writings and their political actions contributed to the making of a new state, even though the major powers of the day prevented its appearance on the international stage: the colonial powers, Apolinario Mabini claimed, knew that the revolution was 'very contagious'.[9] The sense of nationhood, even if it had not penetrated much beyond the elite, at least provided a framework for the relationship with the Americans.

The Philippines had been connected with the outer world, not only by way of its culture, and especially its religion, but also economically. Initially the main link was a novel one for Southeast Asia. Like the Portuguese and later the Dutch, the Spaniards were interested in the fine spices of Maluku; they were also interested in the missionary fields of China and Japan. But they came to concentrate on the Philippines itself so far as missionary activity was concerned, and on Manila's entrepot potential so far as commerce was concerned. 'This trade is so great and profitable and easy to control that the Spaniards do not apply themselves to, or engage in, any other industry', Antonio de Morga wrote in 1609.[10] The novel feature was the trade across the Pacific, conducted by the famous galleons. In Manila the silver of New Spain purchased the luxuries of China. That trade fell away with the independence of the American colonies. Already, indeed, pushed by the British conquest of Manila in 1762, the Spaniards had sought to modernise the Philippines economy and establish a link with Europe via the Cape of Good Hope. Though a Royal Philippine Company was set up, commercial development was mainly left to the foreigners. The export of rice, hemp and sugar linked the Philippines with Australia, Europe and the US, and along the routes of that commerce books, people and ideas also travelled.

The American regime revived and intensified economic ties with US that had been diminishing. While they thought in political terms of autonomy and ultimate independence, the Americans tied the economy of the Philippines closely to markets in the US by tariff concessions and quotas. In particular, Philippines sugar enjoyed a protected market that sustained an important section of the elite and made it difficult to envisage that the islands could stand on their own.

Somewhat paradoxically, however, that close economic connexion came to threaten the political connexion. In the depression the privileged competition of Philippines sugar was resented in the US, and prompted the fixing of a schedule for Philippines independence. In 1916 the Jones Act had promised independence when the islands were ready, but no timetable had been set. In the 1920s the Republicans were less forthcoming than the

Democrats, and concluded that the Philippines was not ready. The new approach was questioned by the Republican President Hoover. But under the Democrat F. D. Roosevelt a new act was passed in 1934. It set up the Commonwealth of the Philippines. At the end of ten years it would become an independent state. Meanwhile its economic privilege would diminish.

Establishing US control in the Philippines helped to preserve the colonial system elsewhere in Southeast Asia: it gave the greatest power in the world an interest in the system, even though it developed a timetabled approach to independence which it wanted other powers to imitate. It stood in the way of Japanese penetration. But once the Japanese decided that they had to secure the resources of Netherlands India by force, the Philippines were drawn into the struggle that ensued: they could not be by-passed.

Japan had less impact on the Philippines than on Indonesia, for independence was already in prospect. It did not therefore have a role in unifying the nationalists or preparing them to oppose the return of the colonial power. Indeed it tended to divide the elite. Some collaborated with the Japanese, some did not. But even that fitted in with the intra-elite struggles that already marked Philippines political life rather than causing any deep discontinuity. At most it helped to produce a 'one-and-a-half' party system, in Onofre Corpuz's phrase, in the postwar period. It also tended to open the way to a left-wing guerilla movement in some parts of Luzon. But the elite proved strong enough to prevent its gaining political power, though not to suppress it altogether.

Whether the Philippines was in these circumstances ready for independence was, however, beside the point. It was important for the US to signal that war had not deflected it from its purpose: the timetable should be implemented, and independence was proclaimed on 4 July 1946. Achieving that, the Americans took a further step towards the consolidation of the elite's control. Their economic policy had led that way. So had their gradual democratisation of politics. MacArthur had recognised Roxas as the strong man of the future, and helped him win the presidency.[11]

The Philippines emerged as an independent state, the first state in Southeast Asia to gain or regain its independence of the colonial powers. But it was a qualified independence. 'I would not for one moment dispute that the retention of American bases in the Philippines is as much to our interest as to the American', Lord Killearn, Britain's Special Commissioner in Southeast Asia, wrote on 7 July 1946. 'It is likewise true that the Filipinos, dependent as they are on the Americans, have bowed to the inevitable with a good grace. But when they discover that the trappings of sovereignty of themselves avail little, it would not be surprising if the Filipinos were to chafe at the restrictions they have now so blithely accepted.'[12] Not only did the US retain bases in the Philippines, which, as in 1941, at once increased its security and reduced it. The US also required the new state to grant American citizens equal opportunity in developing its resources, and to that end, indeed, the Filipinos had to modify their constitution. By contrast to most Southeast Asian countries, the Philippines had undergone major destruction in the war: like Burma, but unlike other territories, it had been fought over, not once, but twice. Rehabilitation was its due. The payment of the large sums involved was also conditioned on constitutional amendment, and on tying the peso to the dollar. And the elite needed that money to consolidate its hold on patronage and its 'pork-barrel' ability to manipulate the electoral system. Roxas, who had gambled on it, found it was insufficient.[13]

That deal qualified the example the Philippines was able to set as an independent state. So, too, did its longer history, which seemed to set it apart from the rest of Southeast Asia. Earlier nationalists had tried to assert the connexion, declaring Rizal to be the pride of the Malay race. Even the claim to Sabah, taken up in the 1920s, was in some sense an attempt to associate or re-associate the Philippines with the rest of the Malay world. That enjoyed little response. The embattled Indonesians were not convinced that the Filipinos had won their independence, nor indeed that it was real.

Filipinos themselves remained torn between the advantages of the American connexion and the humiliation. Under Elpidio Quirino, Roxas's successor, they sought to present themselves as a bridge between East and West, between the US and Asia. In the 1950s American intervention increased in an attempt to counter Huk insurgency, built on peasant protest against Luzon landlordism and on the elitist character of the political system. Filipino nationalism could not but be stirred by this reminder that somehow independence was qualified; yet the US offered security against neighbouring China, Communist after 1949. The Philippines governments tended to use nationalist feelings, again paradoxically, to buy better terms from the Americans for the use of bases, or to extend privileged access to US markets. A further paradox followed. When it became clear that the colony of Sabah would become part of the new federation of Malaysia, the Philippines formalised their claim to the territory. They were at once asserting that they were part of the Malay world and entering a contest with their newly independent neighbour.

The main focus of Philippine politics, however, remained domestic. There were two main parties, but their programmes did not differ. What was important was the distribution of patronage and of the 'pork barrel', by which leaders at all levels rewarded their followers' loyalty. That at least guaranteed a measure of responsiveness, as did the activities of a very free press. But the growth of executive power, foreshadowed in the presidency of the popular Magsaysay in the 1950s, undermined Congress, and that made it easier for Ferdinando Marcos, who had already unprecedentedly won two successive elections, to establish a dictatorial martial law regime in 1972. The promises he held out were not realised. Electoral politics were restored after he was overthrown in 1986. ●

1   *Philippines Herald*, 26 November.
2   G. Saunders, *A History of Brunei*, Kuala Lumpur: Oxford University Press, 1994, p. 45.
3   Felix M. Keesing, *The Ethnohistory of Northern Luzon*, Stanford: Stanford University Press, 1962, p. 45.
4   N. Tarling, ed., *Mrs Pryer in Sabah*, Auckland: Centre for Asian Studies, 1989, pp. 102–3.
5   Marius B. Jansen, *The Japanese and Sun Yat-sen*, Cambridge, Mass: Harvard University Press, 1954, p. 71.
6   Vic Hurley, *Swish of the Kris*, New York: Dutton, 1936, pp. 224–30.
7   *Report on the Conditions of the Philippines in 1842*, reprint, Manila: Historical Conservation Society, 1963, p. 194.
8   E. Alzona, *A History of Education in the Philippines*, Manila: University of Philippines, 1932, pp. 143–4.
9   quoted C. A. Majul, *The Political and Constitutional Ideas of the Philippine Revolution*, Quezon City: University of Philippines, 1957, p. 80.
10 quoted W. L. Schurz, *The Manila Galleon*, New York: Dutton, 1939, p. 39.
11 Lewis E. Gleeck Jr., *Dissolving the Colonial Bond: American Ambassadors to the Philippines, 1946–1984*, Quezon City: New Day, 1988, p. 15.
12 Telegram, 7///46, 28 Saving. FO371/54344 [F10678/10035/83], Public Record Office, London.
13 R. Edgerton, 'The Politics of Reconstruction in the Philippines, 1945–1948', PhD thesis, University of Michigan, 1975, pp. 339–40, 348.

BURMA/MYANMAR

The states of the mainland have enjoyed a continuous historical role for far longer than those in the archipelago. They have not, however, possessed the same frontiers as they do now, even perhaps the same concept of a frontier. Nor have they perceived relations with other states in the contemporary way. They have, like their neighbours in the archipelago, thus passed through a number of historical processes, even though they are not identical. For all but one of them (Thailand) those included the loss of their political independence and their subordination to a colonial power, and their connexion, economically and in other ways, with a wider world than they had hitherto known. Such larger changes, however, were combined with long continuities. The mainland states indeed possess peculiar features, which subsist throughout their history. The problems they face, and the approaches they adopt, have a historical as well as a contemporary dimension. They emerge as states among the states of the post-colonial world with a sense of identity and a sense of continuity which the states of the archipelago do not have. It is indeed tempting for their inhabitants, also for observers, to over-emphasise the continuities and to underestimate the change that has taken place, or that ought to take place.

The Burma state is recognisable in history during the eleventh century CE: the first truly Burman dynasty was established at Pagan in 1054. Its nucleus was the Burman people, but the territory now occupied by Burma (Myanmar) was not unoccupied. The incursion and settlement of the Burmans began a struggle with other peoples which continued with varying degrees of intensity throughout the succeeding centuries into the post-colonial period. Burma, unlike Indonesia, thus had a long history as a state, but it is a state almost always in contention with neighbouring states and political entities. Burma passed through various political formulations, monarchy, colony, republic, democratic or authoritarian. All had different formulae for dealing with this fundamental issue.

The peoples with whom the Burmans contended included the Mons, pushed towards the south, yet remaining a formidable force. The founder of the last Burman dynasty, Alaungpaya, defeated them in 1752, and founded a new city, Rangoon (Yangon), optimistically believing it marked 'the end of strife'. Yet the Mons remained active. The British asked themselves whether they should seek their help when they went to war with the Burmans: would that subject them to a worse fate if they then withdrew? When the British state itself came to an end 140 years later, the Mons made a bid for a political role in its successor, albeit in vain. 'Even if there were a case for doing something for the Mons at the Constituent Assembly,' A. F. Morley commented at the Burma Office in London, 'it would be quite impracticable . . . to do anything for them in the elections for the CA.'[1]

The peoples with whom the Burmans contended also included those in the hills, Kachins, Chins, and Shans. There they often managed to reach an understanding based on mutual recognition: the chiefs would accept what Europeans might call the suzerainty of the Burman king; but he would permit them a great deal of autonomy. They would be a peripheral rather than a central part of the Burma state. That relationship was not free of violence, but it offered a balanced relationship not unacceptable to both sides. A reorganisation of the state of Burma, however, might make it difficult to sustain. A colonial state might draw up more rigid frontiers and extend its writ within them more firmly. A state, colonial or independent, in which there were parliamentary elections was likely to produce within those frontiers a majority–minority relationship far more tense than the relationship between king and chiefs.

Yet another case was the relationship between the Burmans and the Karens. The Karens were hill peoples, but some also came to the plains. That presented a double challenge to post-monarchical Burma. Even if a frontier could more or less be drawn between Burman and Karen lands, a minority of Karens would remain within majority Burman territory. Furthermore a number of Karens became Christian, as a result of their response to the American Baptist missionaries, and thus further distinguished themselves from the predominantly Buddhist Burmans.

Burma's response to the outer world was indeed shaped by these antagonisms. Asserting control over neighbouring peoples, the Burman monarch was assertive in regard to foreigners wider afield as well. They could be seen as subverting his authority over the peoples under his suzerainty. Those peoples, like the Mons and Karens, might indeed look for and welcome help against the Burmans. The assertiveness, but also the apprehension, helps to explain the combative relationship with the Thai state. It also helps to explain the relationship with the British. That brought about three wars, in 1824–6, 1852, and 1885, the piecemeal loss of territory to the colonial power, and the final destruction of the kingdom in 1886.

In the colonial phase that ensued, Burman nationalism took shape in response to the changes that the British brought. It naturally focused its antagonism on the British, and also on the Indians, many of whom entered Burma from the British empire in India and took up opportunities that the new British administration in Burma, an extension of that in India, opened up. But even so the older antagonisms did not disappear. The non-Burman peoples had a different place in the colonial state, a different place again when an electoral system was introduced in it. Some, like the Karens, were to develop their own national aspirations. Tenasserim, San C. Po argued in 1928, should be administered by Karens: ' "Karen Country," how inspiring it sounds! What thoughts, what manly feeling, what wonderful visions of the future the words conjure forth in the mind of a Karen.'[2] But to the Burmans themselves it seemed that the colonial power was adopting the old maxim, divide and rule.

It had, of course, acquired the land of the Burmans itself stage by stage, Arakan and Tenasserim after the first war, Pegu after the second, the remnant of the kingdom and its claims over the Shans and others after the third. That meant that the Burmans had an experience of the British or British rule that was differentiated chronologically. But if the length of exposure to the changes that British and British-Indian rule brought were varied, the thrust of that rule did not greatly vary from region to region.

Furthermore, the kingdom itself endured, albeit over a diminished territory, till the 1880s. The reaction to the British was marked by a strong sense of Burman unity and a vivid recollection of monarchical rule.

Western-style nationalism interrelated with an older sense of unity, 'a traditional Burmese nationalism arising from Burma's cultural homogeneity',[3] in some sense strengthening it, in some sense diversifying, even weakening it. That was not merely because it emphasised the distinct identity of non-Burman peoples. It also introduced new dichotomies among the Burmans themselves. The spread of Western education prompted the adoption of Western organisational forms. A Young Men's Buddhist Association was, for example, both imitation of and counter to the YMCA. The organisation of political parties followed, with the advent of participatory political structures after the First World War. There were, of course, differences among the Western-educated elite, which such parties articulated: they indeed tended to be factions, leaders and followers, patrons and clients, with little ideological differentiation. None could claim not to be working for the prompt grant of greater autonomy, if not independence. The only difference could be over the extent to which that might be achieved by collaboration with the British.

There, indeed, other differences made themselves felt. To some extent those resulted from the other dichotomies brought to Burma by the mingling of older traditions of unity and newer forms of nationalism. Opposition to British rule, to the intrusion of the West more generally, to the migration of the Indians, did not merely take the modern nationalist forms that in some sense British rule introduced. The fall of the monarchy was recent, and popular resistance to foreign rule was often manifested in would-be monarchical forms, evident, for example, in the climactic Saya San rebellion of 1930–1. Opposition was also led by the *pongyi*, the Buddhist monks who, deprived even of the organisational structure of the old monarchy, retained, even increased, their hold on Burman society. Few politicians could neglect them. The extent to which they felt it necessary to rely on them would determine their capacity to take part in the constitutional experiments of the British in the inter-war period.

Those experiments were designed to promote the political advance of Burma, ultimately, it was agreed, towards the Dominion status in the empire enjoyed by Canada, Australia and New Zealand. The chances that this programme would succeed were, however, limited. The British began it rather reluctantly. It derived from promises made to India towards the end of the war, rather than from promises made to Burma. In 1917 Montagu, the Secretary of State, envisaged 'the gradual development of self-governing institutions, with a view to the progressive realisation of responsible government in India as an integral part of the British Empire'.[4] The concept was extended to Burma, then part of the Indian empire, only because of Burman pressure. Even then, the Burmans were divided as to whether they should cooperate or not, legitimising the programme by their participation, or standing apart, as the *pongyi* urged, and as popular feeling suggested. The result was ambiguous.

The reforms themselves enhanced the ambiguity of their effect. They were based on the principle of dyarchy: there would be an increasing degree of executive responsibility to an increasingly elected assembly. Some spheres of government would be made over to Burmans, who might be in something of the position of 'ministers'. But under such a system there could be no cabinet responsibility. Nor, indeed, could there be a government with an overall programme. The experiment, though designed to give experience of the parliamentary system, did not do so and could not do so. It was hard for such a system to win over those who doubted the validity of the whole experiment. Those who took part found it hard to work. How could parties be organised around a programme if no government could implement one? Political support had to be built by money, by patronage, and increasingly by paramilitary activity. And there could be no objective other than to aim at independence.

There was another ambiguity. Burma had been acquired as a bastion of the empire in India, and Indian immigration expanded. Resentment of this presence occurred at several levels of Burmese society, firing both the nationalism of the educated elite, and the anti-foreign resentment of peasants who found their land falling into the hands of Indian moneylenders and of urban workers who found themselves displaced or pre-empted. Yet it was the advance of India towards self-government that had prompted the British to consider its extension to Burma, and while Burman pressure had also been required, Burman nationalists believed that they still needed Indian support and example. They found themselves in a quandary in the early 1930s, when further advance was being considered. Separation from India was the obvious goal for a would-be independent Burma. But if it came too soon, the British might be able to hold Burma back even though India advanced. The struggle involved other paradoxes: the anti-separationist campaign was supported by Indians in Burma, nationalist politicians thus boosting their electoral funds. The British decided on separation. In fact the Burmans got the constitution of 1935–7 going, whereas that in India did not get off the ground.

The Burma constitution was a more democratic one than any elsewhere in Southeast Asia at the time, more indeed than that in the Philippines. But it had no good answer to the problem of representing the minorities, since, like other electoral systems, the Burma constitution tended both at once to entrench them and to marginalise them. Nor did it cover all Burma. The 'scheduled areas', mainly the 'fringe' inhabited by Shans, Kachins, Chins, and some of the Karens, remained directly under the governor, rather than under the parliamentary system. That was a source of frustration to Burman nationalists, along with their distaste for the remnants of British control in parliamentary Burma, and their resentment of the role of the Indians. They also focused on the major European enterprises in oil, mining, timber and transportation: they seemed to extract too much and offer too little in return.

The more extreme nationalists, led by the student politicians of the 1930s and calling themselves Thakins, played with left-wing ideas, but took the opportunity offered by the incursion of the Japanese. Contact was made even before the attack, and during the occupation a Thakin-led Burma Defence Army cooperated with the Japanese and a puppet regime, headed by Ba Maw, was given independence in 1943. As the tide of war turned, the Thakin leadership determined to secure independence. The Burma Defence Army, led by Aung San, offered to collaborate with the British, and the offer was accepted. That put the Thakin political organisation, the Anti-Fascist People's Freedom League (AFPFL), in a strong position when British administration was restored after the re-conquest and sought to implement the policy of the White Paper of May 1945. In fact, the British never fully regained control, and in 1947 the AFPFL secured a promise of independence. The British sought to guarantee the position of the minority peoples, some of whom had fought on their side earlier in the war. But what they gained was insufficient to prevent widespread insurrection on their part within a few months of the establishment of the Union, independent and outside the Commonwealth, on 4 January 1948; first it was the Karens, then others.

The Union government survived, though it seemed at first that it might not. Democratic politics did not survive. The government was beset not only by continuing opposition from Communists, Karens and hill peoples. It also faced economic problems that outlasted the Korean war boom, and the socialist approach of the AFPFL did nothing to attract foreign capital. Divisions within the AFPFL increased, and the military leadership seized its opportunity to take over, first of all on a temporary basis, and then more permanently. By contrast to the military regime in Indonesia, that in Burma was not development-oriented. Its own concern to retain power was combined with an extreme version of the anti-foreign socialism of the earlier years. Challenged in the late eighties the military regime reaffirmed its control, while beginning to seek foreign investment and support. ●

---

1   Minute, 23/1/47, M/4/2542, India Office Library, London.

2   San C. Po, *Burma and the Karens*, London: Elliot Stock, 1928, p. 81.

3   Aung San Suu Kyi, *Freedom from Fear*, Harmondsworth: Penguin, 1995, p. 105.

4   quoted T. G. P. Spear, *India: A Modern History*, Ann Arbor: Michigan University Press, 1961, pp. 342–3.

VIETNAM

The Burmans' sense of unity grew in the course of their contacts and conflicts with neighbouring peoples well before they faced the incursion of the British and the Indians. The Vietnamese sense of unity derived from an initial conflict with a dominant power, imperial China. Vietnam won its independence from that power in the tenth century partly because it had been colonised by it and had borrowed from it, a paradox that in some sense parallels the winning of independence by nationalist movements in the phase of European colonialism. Chinese rule in Vietnam had restructured society and given it, as it were, weapons that were turned against it, and used again when the Ming re-established the province of Giao-chi in 1407. Le Loi (Le Thai-to) turned out the 'mad Ming'. 'O, but one warrior's coat has set up a Great Order. An unprecedented task has been accomplished. The Four Seas shall be quiet forever. An era of renovation shall be announced in every place.'[1]

The Vietnamese state thus created and re-created was a much smaller state than the Vietnam of the European phase or its present-day successor. But it was in part the coherence given it by Chinese rule and by the resistance to Chinese rule that enabled it to expand southwards at the expense of other peoples, including the Chams, whose kingdom was virtually destroyed by 1471 CE, and the Khmers, who were pushed into the Mekong delta and then out of that, too, with the founding of Saigon at the end of the seventeenth century. Moreover, the Vietnamese people retained a sense of unity during their colonising process. It was not a sense of nationhood in the Western sense. But it had some of its features, some features indeed that not all nationalisms have; those included a common language and a powerful if localised sense of community.

Nevertheless, such patterns, developed in the north, were difficult to replicate further south, and as the realm and the people expanded there, they were modified. What worked in the relatively densely populated Red River delta – the core of which was the commune or *xa* – was not entirely appropriate for the more tropical frontier lands of the Mekong. These differences challenged Vietnamese political genius, too. So, indeed, did another geographical factor. The realm came to seem like two baskets on a pole, represented by the thin strip of coastal territory that makes up central Vietnam. Was it possible for the sense of unity the Vietnamese still had to be complemented and supported by a political unity? If so, of what kind should it be?

Once the realm reached beyond the boundaries of the late fifteenth century, political unity came into question. The seventeenth century was particularly marked by civil war. The main figures had begun as lords of the palace for the Le dynasty, but they became rival territorial rulers under that dynasty's ineffectual suzerainty. The Trinh ruled in most of the old heartland of the Vietnamese, their capital Hanoi (Thanh-long). The Nguyen family ruled the lands to the south of Song-Gianh, newer acquisitions for the most part, from their capital at Hué. The war did not, however, stop Vietnamese expansion at the expense of others. Rather the reverse was true. Seeking additional resources to maintain their autonomy, if not to defeat their northern rivals, the Nguyen continued the advance to Saigon and beyond, now at the expense of the Khmers.

It was with a politically divided Vietnam that the Europeans made contact, and their contact may have promoted division. For the Portuguese and the Dutch were seen as sources of weapons in the civil war, and other kinds of trade were a secondary consideration. With the end of the civil war – a stalemate was reached in the 1670s along the 18° parallel and a wall built – the Dutch lost much of their importance. Missions sponsored by the Jesuits and the Société des Missions Etrangères had a more long-term impact. France, not a commercial power, nevertheless sought to play a role in Asia. Promoting missionary activity was one of the tasks the French assumed, and, untouched by Islam, and less absorbed than the Thais and the Burmans by Theravada Buddhism, the Vietnamese proved responsive, especially in the north. But the regime itself saw missionary activities as subversive, and Christian communities, though surviving, were distrusted.

The dynamics of Vietnam's history in the eighteenth century were traditional, in that they were not the result of outsiders' activities, nor even of responses to them. The pressures that the two regimes exerted on the population, particularly, it seems, that of the Nguyen, produced the great revolt that the brothers from Tay-son led in the 1770s. That culminated in a new attempt to reaffirm the political unity of Vietnam, replacing the Le dynasty, in whose name the Trinh and the Nguyen had ruled, by a revolutionary dynasty. It did not survive. It was challenged by the Chinese whose intervention was repulsed in 1788. But it was also challenged from the south by a revived Nguyen leadership. It was the Nguyen in the event who re-established Vietnam's unity, and Nguyen Anh proclaimed himself the Emperor Gia-long in 1802.

In these moves there had been some foreign participation. Nguyen Anh had sought aid from the French, and a treaty had been made at Versailles in 1787. In fact little effective aid was forthcoming, and the victory of the Nguyen was largely of their own making. In any case, once Vietnam was re-unified, the regime was at pains to reduce foreign influence. That was seen as associated with civil war and division. Moreover, the regime determined to rebuild its unity on the basis of the Confucian principles it had borrowed from China. Under Gia-long's successor, Minh-Mang, that became even more the case, irrelevant though much of Chinese precept and practice was to a much smaller state, the southern part of which at least was diverse and polyglot. Giving reality to the Vietnamese sense of unity remained a political challenge for the rulers. Their answer was once more to reaffirm the validity of what Alexander Woodside has called the 'Chinese model'.[2]

Doing this brought tensions within Vietnam. It also provoked conflict with the West. It made it impossible to respond positively to the approaches of the British, even after the Anglo-China war of 1840–2 had shown the dangers of a negative response. That left the way open to a renewal of the French interest in Vietnam, and the French were more likely to act in Vietnam just because the British were so successful in China. The Nguyen rulers gave them an opportunity. 'It so happened that the Vietnamese were stubborn and determined to hold on to their old policy', as King Mongkut of Siam put it. 'They did not know the real strength of the maritime powers and there was nobody to tell them of the real might and custom of these distant lands.'[3] Re-affirming the Chinese model prompted Vietnamese antagonism to Christian missionary activity, evident under Minh-mang and his successors. Even in the 1840s French naval vessels, in the area as a result of the China war, were intervening in Vietnam in support of the missionaries whom the regime sought to drive out. In the 1850s Napoleon III made a bid for Catholic support for his 'Second Empire' at home by taking up the missionary cause in Vietnam. Britain's involvement with the Indian Mutiny seemed a good time to act, while the decapitation of a Spanish bishop offered a good opportunity for seeking the collaboration of the Spaniards in the Philippines. In 1858 a Franco-Spanish expedition attacked Danang, and the following year Saigon was occupied. Allowed a great deal of latitude by the authorities in Paris, the French naval authorities secured control of several southern provinces, and a colony of Cochin-China was created. The British offered no opposition. Vietnam had not established positive relations with them, and they were not apprehensive over the French venture, so long as it did not encroach on the independence of Siam.

In subsequent years, indeed, the French expanded their control over the rest of Vietnam. The Second Empire had fallen in face of the German invasion of France in 1870; but the Third Republic took up its colonial ventures all the more strongly, indeed, because of France's defeat in Europe and the need to demonstrate, to Frenchmen as well as to the world at large, that France was still great. The weakness of the Nguyen regime, coupled with the hostility that the French had aroused, meant that there were plenty of opportunities for combative Frenchmen to seize. Jules Ferry put the authority of the French state behind them. In 1883 the French established a protectorate over Vietnam, and after a conflict with the Chinese asserted their control over Tonkin.

The Nguyen had not been able to mobilise the people they ruled against the European conquerors. Initially they had hoped to negotiate the departure of the French. More generally they seemed to be apprehensive about unleashing anti-foreign feeling that might focus upon the dynasty as well. The French were able to find collaborators and to set up a puppet emperor. Only in the last crisis did the Ham-Nghi emperor seek to put himself at the head of the resistance. Traditional resistance, however, continued well into the 1890s.

As in other Southeast Asian countries, the European rulers, albeit largely involuntarily, helped to modernise the movements that opposed the continuance of their rule. Some Vietnamese looked to Japan, where empire and modernity had combined. Others recognised that the Vietnamese had to learn from the French. Collaborationists could indeed justify the course they took in this way. Phan Chu Trinh and the reformists and Phan Boi Chau and the activists were 'essentially two factions of the same anticolonialist movement'.[4] Others, without openly collaborating, yet absorbed French political ideas. Though the French in the colonies did not apply them, that made them more relevant, rather than less so. The educational opportunities the French made available were very limited, and the political opportunities non-existent. Even so, the traditional sense of unity among the Vietnamese was re-shaped by modern nationalism.

It was also shaped by Communism. Again, this was of European origin. Its aims were at odds with nationalism, and indeed in some sense in competition. In face of opposition, however, the opposites could join, their differences not abandoned, but suppressed for a time. In two of the Southeast Asian colonies, that ruled by the Dutch and that ruled by the French, Communism played a substantial and continued role. That derived partly from its role in the metropolitan territories. In Netherlands India, it took root also partly because there was a receptive Dutch and European element in the colony which became a means of transmission. What emerged was, to use Sjahrir's words, 'a strange sort of Communism indeed'.[5] In Vietnam Communism took root because of contacts with the metropolis and because of the proximity of China. But the failure of the French regime to offer any scope to moderate nationalist movements tended to drive nationalists into extreme positions, and to give the Communists an opportunity to assume their leadership. 'Where fear drove the French administration to reject any significant liberalization of their rule, the middle ground of genuine constitutional opposition of the sort which emerged in India was not available.'[6] The bitterest clashes occurred in the depression. The Yen-bay mutinies were put down with great violence, and the Nghe-an Soviets brutally crushed. The French did not hesitate to invoke air-power, rarely used in colonial territories.

The Japanese phase in Vietnam was both shorter and longer than elsewhere. Defeated in Europe, the French came to terms with Japan in 1940–41, but they were not actually displaced till early in 1945. The occupation did not, therefore, give the nationalists much scope, and the Tran Trong Kim regime was, moreover, not allowed to take over the colony of Cochin-China until the eve of the Japanese surrender in August. The Communists seized their opportunity. The Viet-minh proclaimed the independence of Vietnam in Hanoi on the very day of the formal surrender in Tokyo, 2 September.

Like the other colonial powers, the French sought to re-establish themselves. In the south, they received from the British more direct help than the Dutch did in Java. In the north, where the KMT Chinese were the occupying power, they had to compromise with the Viet-minh, which was in any case stronger in Tonkin than in Cochin-China. Their partial success, however, encouraged the French to think that they could avoid further compromise, and even retreat from the compromise they had made. That negative approach was also prompted by the approach of the men on the spot, in particularly the Gaullist High Commissioner, Admiral Thierry d'Argenlieu, and by the absence of control from Paris. In Paris, governments were distracted and ephemeral. It was impossible to develop a forward-looking policy that might have had a chance, even at this stage, of both accommodating and succouring a moderate Vietnamese nationalism. The way was left open to those who believed that French authority could now be restored by the means through which it had been earlier sustained, a mixture of short-term violence and the recruitment of collaborators. That strategy could no longer work. Instead it consolidated the Communist leadership of the nationalist movement.

Belatedly and indeed half-heartedly the French sought to establish 'the Bao Dai regime', rule by the Nguyen emperor, though without his being installed as emperor. Its position was, however, ambiguous not only with respect to the past, but with respect to the present. The French were reluctant to grant it a share of power that would convince the Vietnamese that it really was or could soon become an independent Vietnamese state and thus embody the hopes and attract the support of nationalists who did not care for the Communist alternative. The French, wrote John Street at the British Foreign Office in 1948, did not 'really envisage handing over any authority to Annamites (perhaps because of the reactions in North Africa), and this attitude will continue to hamstring their efforts to establish security in Indo-China'.[7]

The defeat of the French in 1954 and the Geneva agreements led to a de facto partition of Vietnam along a line not far from that which had once divided the Trinh and Nguyen lands. The Americans came to support the southern regime, dominated at first by a Catholic mandarin, Ngo Dinh Diem, who displaced Bao Dai. But, whatever the failings of its rulers, a merely southern regime had few chances of long-term survival. At most it might have been a stage in the reconstitution of a unified Vietnam, the ideal that had often evaded the Vietnamese. The Viet-minh and its supporters in the south undermined the regime's local support, and no amount of bombardment of the north could win it respite. The compromise finally negotiated in 1973 was thus very much in favour of the Viet-minh. The regime in the south was soon overrun. ●

---

1   A Great Proclamation upon the Pacification of the Wu, 1428, quoted Truong Buu Lam, *Patterns of Vietnamese Response to Foreign Intervention*, New Haven: Southeast Asia Studies, Yale University Press, 1967, p. 61.

2   A. B. Woodside, *Vietnam and the Chinese Model*, Cambridge, Mass.: Harvard University Press, 1971.

3   Mongkut/Norodom, 1865. quoted Neon Snidvongs, 'The development of Siamese relations with Britain and France in the reign of Maha Mongkut', PhD thesis, London University, 1961, p. 209.

4   P. Baugher, 'The Contradictions of Colonialism: the French Experience in Indochina, 1860–1940', PhD, University of Wisconsin–Madison, 1980, p. 280.

5   quoted Bruce Grant, *Indonesia*, Melbourne: Melbourne University Press, 1964, p. 21.

6   M. Osborne, in W. F. Vella, ed., *Aspects of Vietnamese History*, Honolulu: Hawaii University Press, 1973, p. 167.

7   Minute, 20/1/48. FO371/69653B [F943/255/86].

SIAM/THAILAND

Like the Burmans and the Vietnamese, but unlike the peoples of the Malay world, the Thais sustained a tradition of political unity well before the advent of the nation-state. Unlike the former, but again unlike those of the Malay world, they did not in the meantime undergo the experience of colonial rule. Their experience was thus unique. But to some extent their unity, like that of the Burmans and the Vietnamese, was built out of contention with their neighbours as well as borrowings from them. Nor were the colonial powers without an impact. The Thai kingdom took on some of the features of the colonial territories that surrounded it, partly in order to limit the acquisitions the Europeans made at its expense. It also began to build up Thai nationalism, based in part on its traditions, based also on latter-day antagonisms, though often directed more at the Chinese than at the colonial powers.

From 1352 the Thai kingdom enjoyed a positional advantage that the Burmans, and, to a still greater extent, the Vietnamese, lacked. The Thais came to occupy the basin of the great river, Menam Chaophraya, and they placed their capital near its mouth, first at Ayuthia, and later further down, at Bangkok. That had a drawback. Those parts of the kingdom that were peripheral to the river system, marginally or completely beyond its limits, would tend to escape the control of the capital, whether they were on the Malay Peninsula or in the northeast plateau, Isan. But it also had an advantage. Establishing a capital at the mouth of the river enabled the rulers to regulate most of the Thais' contacts with the outer world. It also helped the rulers to inform themselves about the outer world. The contrast with rulers in Pagan and in Hué was pointed.

As they extended south, the Thais borrowed from the ancient Khmer kingdom they helped to displace. They also assimilated the Theravada Buddhism, originating in Sri Lanka, that they shared with the Burmans. The foundations for their monarchy were thus laid, elaborated and built upon by outstanding rulers like King Trailokanat.

> The progressive elaboration of the system of labour control conceived during his reign became the basis for the regenerative if not enduring strength of Ayutthaya in following centuries... It meant that the traditional Tai practice of personal patron-client relationships would henceforth be interacting with a more bureaucratic and impersonal system of control. Very likely, the administrative reforms of Trailok were inspired by the legacy of Angkor.[1]

The sense of unity was also articulated and intensified by conflict with neighbouring peoples. The Khmers were the least formidable of their foes, and the Cambodian kingdom survived only because it was able to turn its position between Thais and Vietnamese to account. The Thais pressed south into the peninsula, particularly when the Malay states were weakened by the incursions of the Portuguese and the Dutch. But their main antagonists were the Burmans. The assertiveness of new Burman dynasties helped to generate conflict, the climax of which was the destruction of Ayuthia in 1767. The Thais recovered quickly. Their new state was stronger than the old, more assertive in regard to its neighbours, even more alive to the advantages of regulated contact with the outside world.

It was this state that now had to deal with the colonialism of the nineteenth century. There had, of course, been earlier contacts with the Europeans. Neither the Portuguese nor the Dutch had been a serious threat to Ayuthia. At one time, it seemed that the French, supporting the missions in Vietnam, would also be able to dominate the Thai capital. Their embassy of 1685 was at first well received, but then they were turned out, and Phaulkon, the Greek adventurer who had encouraged them, was executed. The Bangkok dynasty, however, reasserted Thai unity and revived Thai ambitions at the very time that the British were expanding their control in

India and pursuing their interests beyond it with greater vigour. The Sultan of Kedah, in making over Penang to the East India Company, was looking for support against the Thais, and in the subsequent decades, when they in fact occupied Kedah, a conflict with the British seemed possible. It was avoided not only by British restraint, but by the Thais' caution, born in part of the sense of reality that long-standing contact with the outer world brought them. The company and the Thai kingdom concluded the Burney Treaty in 1826.

Dealing with the Europeans indeed involved making what the Chinese would term 'unequal treaties'. The British were far from anxious to extend their empire, and rather looked towards sustaining the Thai kingdom as a marcher territory on their frontiers, and later as a buffer between their possessions and those of the French. They did, however, insist on commercial opportunities in Thailand, and to that end in 1855 secured extraterritorial jurisdiction and limits on Thai customs duties. The Thais also made territorial concessions to the Europeans as a price of continued independence. Fortunately, perhaps, European imperialism came at a time when the kingdom had reached its greatest extent. It was thus possible to concede territories that were on the margins – in Laos, Cambodia, on the peninsula – and not part of the core of the kingdom. 'It is sufficient for us to keep ourselves within our house and home', Mongkut had said in 1867; 'it may be necessary for us to forego some of our former power and influence.'[2]

This diplomacy was a testimony to the skill of rulers like Mongkut. But it might also be seen as a testimony to the strength of the kingdom rather than as a testimony to the strength of national feeling. Indeed, had such a feeling existed, it would have been much harder to make territorial bargains with colonial powers, even in respect of territories that were not predominantly Thai. The kingdom was able to behave in a sense like a colonial power, taking more account of commercial and strategic interests than of ethnic or national loyalites. Undoubtedly, however, it was important that the territories ceded were often Khmer or Malay. Yielding up a great part of Laos to the Third French Republic was a rather different matter, for Laos and Thais were more closely affiliated.

Even so, it was the monarchy that took the initiative in attempting to preserve the state, not merely by concession, but by modernisation: 'One of the surest means of consolidating Siam's external autonomy and independence was to improve prudently but seriously its internal administration', as the Belgian General Adviser, Gustave Rolin-Jaequemyns, put it in 1894.[3] Modernisation was not a policy that had served the Burman monarchy of Mindon or Thibaw, partly because it had led to contacts with other powers that the British could not tolerate. The Thais were in a stronger position. They took care to employ British advisers, but they employed advisers from other countries also, the US and Belgium among others. In foreign affairs their state was to behave like other states, and so be in a position to undo extraterritoriality. At home it was to affirm its unity, in effect by undertaking steps that European colonial rulers were to a greater or lesser extent undertaking elsewhere, building railways and telegraphs, reorganising local administration, extending education. King Chulalongkorn's 'prime models were...the Dutch East/Indies, British Malaya, and the Raj', which he had visited back in 1870 and 1872: government was to be rationalised and centralised, economic development promoted.[4] But J. G. D. Campbell pointed out, from personal experience, that in Siam advisers did not have 'the iron hand in the velvet glove' as in India and Malaya. 'In Siam...an adviser is an adviser and nothing else.'[5]

It was only in this context that a modern sense of nationalism began to emerge. Initially, again, it was encouraged by the monarch. In part it was directed against the Chinese, who had taken up so many of the commercial opportunities that Bangkok offered. Rama VI described them famously (or infamously) as the Jews of Asia. He also sought to evoke a heroic monarchical past, commemorating, for example, 321 years later by a service at the subsequently forgotten stupa he had erected King Naresuan's glorious victory over the Burmans in 1593.[6] In the interwar period Thai nationalism came to encompass a challenge to the West, and in particular to the territorial framework it had imposed on mainland Southeast Asia.

The monarchy had won further concessions from the Western powers by joining in the First World War at the same time as the US and China. At the peace conference, it was able to assert its equality with other states, and in the 1920s to press on with the re-negotiation of the unequal treaties. '...with the growth of education (and the Siamese Government is doing remarkable work in education) a demand for more modern and up-to-date governmental institutions will soon make itself heard even in contented Siam', it was observed at the British Foreign Office, 'and we shall only increase the odium to which we are always exposed in the Far East if, by the time that stage is reached, we remain the one power clinging to the vestiges of a system which is increasingly felt as a humiliation.'[7] Modernisation, indeed, brought a challenge to the absolute monarchy itself. More of the elite had been overseas for higher education, even to France, and the armed forces had been expanded. Many were discontented at the dominance of the king and the princes, and the depression led to the coup of 1932. It did not overthrow the monarchy, but it ended its absolute power. Theoretically it was constitutionalised. In fact power fell into the hands of an oligarchy, made up of civilian and military leaders, generally 'Promoters' of the coup. Increasingly the military elements predominated, above all the ambitious Luang Pibun Songkram, subsequently Prime Minister.

The Promoters did not merely have in mind change at home. They sought to change Thailand's position in the world. The world was itself changing, the colonial powers who dominated Southeast Asia coming under pressure, not only from the Communists, but from the Germans and the Japanese. Initially the Promoters were cautious, apprehensive lest colonial powers should intervene and restore the absolute monarchy with which they had dealt for so long. Of that there was in fact no chance, and, particularly as the military wing gained more prominence, the Thais began to contemplate the reunification of the kingdom in a 'pan-Thai' form. Civilian Promoters were not deaf to the call of nationalism, but preferred a different route, and a more cautious one. Undoubtedly the strident propaganda of Pibun's supporter, Luang Vichit, had its appeal.[8]

The growth of Japan's power and ambition offered both an opportunity and a constraint. Through Japanese pressure on the French, for example, the Thais might be able to regain parts of Laos and Cambodia over which they had earlier been forced to relinquish their claims. But it was better to have a weak France on the frontier than a strong Japan. And, if it were possible even so to gain at France's expense, it ought not to place Thailand under an excessive obligation to Japan. Maybe, however, Japan would be able to dominate Southeast Asia in any case. If the West was to be eliminated, perhaps it was after all best to secure what could be secured, even if it was a gift from Japan. It was not surprising that Pibun's policy was difficult to follow, and perhaps difficult to determine, in the period between the opening of the European war in 1939 and the opening of the Pacific war in 1941. He could not resist the opportunity to take advantage of the fall of France. But Japan imposed a so-called mediation that increased its influence over both sides. Japan, the US ambassador in Tokyo thought, had 'at least laid the groundwork for the political, economic, and presumably eventual military control of Indochina and Thailand'.[9]

Once the war started, Thailand allowed the passage of Japanese forces after only a brief resistance. Soon after it declared war on the Western powers. During the war, it accepted the transfer of the northern Malay states, suzerainty over which had been relinquished to the British in 1909, and it secured two of the Shan states that had formed part of the scheduled areas of the Burma of 1935. It did not acquire more territory in Laos and Cambodia at the expense of the French, who remained in control till March 1945. After March, when the Japanese overthrew them, the Thais were busy attempting to reinsure their position in the face of the approaching victory of the Allies.

There again their diplomacy, as under the absolute monarchy, was discerning. What was important – as, after all, the Vietnamese and the Indonesians recognised – was the attitude of the US. That power had never seen itself as at war with the Thais and, unlike the British, had not had territory it controlled taken over by them. Dropping their military leadership, the Thais were able to rely on the Americans in their attempts to limit the retributive policy of the British. They were not able to retain the territories they had secured under the Japanese, even those in Indo-China, though that was an aspiration of the civilian leadership as well as the military. Nai Pridi Phanomyong, Pibun's civilian rival and Prime Minister 1946–47, offered some support to Indo-China nationalist leaders, and the concept of a Southeast Asia League that was advanced at the time was in some sense an analogue of the pan-Thai policy. But it did not succeed.

In the Cold War world, Pibun and his successors continued a close association with the US, but Thailand was never, in Brailey's view, merely a client.[10] At home, monarchy and Buddhism were set at the basis of the state, though effective power was in the hands of the armed forces. It was out of this Thailand that, somewhat haphazardly, an 'economic tiger' was born. Its infrastructure was weak. But the aspirations of an older nationalism could be detected behind the continuing determination to use its economic power to build a leadership role among the states of the mainland. ●

1   Keith W. Taylor, 'The Early kingdoms', in N. Tarling, ed., *Cambridge History of Southeast Asia* I, Cambridge: Cambridge University Press; 1992, p. 171.

2   quoted A. L. Moffat, *Mongkut, the King of Siam*, Ithaca NY: Cornell University Press, 1961, p. 124.

3   quoted Walter E. J. Tips, *Gustave Rolin-Jaequemyns and the Making of Modern Siam*, Bangkok: White Lotus, 1996, p. 225.

4   B. Anderson, *Imagined Communities*, London and New York: Verso, 1983, pp. 109–110fn.

5   J. G. D. Campbell, *Siam in the Twentieth Century*, London: Arnold, 1902, pp. 168–9.

6   W. F. Vella, *Chaiyo!* Honolulu: Hawaii University Press, 1978, p. 207.

7   FO Memo quoted P. B. Oblas, 'Siam's Efforts to Revise the Unequal Treaty System in the Sixth Reign (1910–1925)', PhD, Michigan University, 1974, p. 232.

8   Scott Barme, *Luang Vichit Wathakan and the creation of a Thai identity*, Singapore: Institute of Southeast Asian Studies, 1993.

9   quoted N. Tarling, *Britain, Southeast Asia and the Onset of the Pacific War*, Cambridge: Cambridge University Press, 1996, p. 266.

10 N. J. Brailey, *Thailand and the Fall of Singapore*, Boulder: Westview, 1986, p. 169.

Part Two

PROBLEMS AND POLICIES

This part of the book takes up a number of topics in Southeast Asian history that may add to the understanding of the emergence of modern states discussed in Part One but also contribute to studying the history of the region as such. The choice of topics is limited, if not idiosyncratic. They focus particularly on the making of Southeast Asian states and on the tensions, fruitful and unfruitful, between East and West that mark their modern history and affect their contemporary position.

COLONIAL AND NATIONAL FRONTIERS

Frontiers are real enough in Western parlance to be the making of metaphor. A frontier is something that is crossed, characteristically from state to state, a line often dividing security from danger, neutrality from war. They are also something that is moved or advanced. They can be drawn on a map. Adjectivally, the word is also applied to those involved, a frontier society, frontiersmen. By way of metaphor, frontier comes to describe other kinds of advance, the social advance of the 'New Frontier', the scholarly advance of pushing back (or forward) the frontiers of knowledge. 'Whoever wants to give his students complete conviction about the accuracy of his statements... must have worked on the boundaries of human knowledge and conquered new worlds for it.'[1]

The concept of a frontier was uncommon, if not unknown, in Southeast Asia. The idea that the ambit of a state was geographically fixed was rarely accepted. What counted in Southeast Asia, sparse in population, was allegiance. Whom, rather than what, did the state comprise? States might indeed advance or retreat, grow or decline, but in terms of adherents and followers, of a network of familial and supra-familial relationships. The spirit of the frontier might be there – Menangkabauers wandered, Iban undertook *bejalai*, too – but that was fitted into a cultural pattern that stressed continuity rather than change.

What concerned a ruler was the people not the place. The sense that the state was a geographical or locational entity was rarely strong. 'Thus a British surveyor trying to demarcate the boundaries of a Malay state in 1875 could elicit no more exact information from the local potentate concerning the limits of his territory than that if you wash your head before starting, it will not be dry before you reach the place.'[2] The place might be relatively inexact. The terms of allegiance of the people concerned would be much more precise. That was the prior consideration: where the people went, there the state went.

Colonial officials had indeed quite a different concept of frontier. Even in respect of the states from which they came, however, it had taken time to develop, and it had still not attained the intensity given it, amidst all their globalism, by the nation-states of the twentieth century. In Europe the frontier was of slow growth, as was the state. The way in which allegiance to the state was determined varied over time. For much of European history it was a matter of feudal allegiance. Only as the state modernised itself was allegiance determined by other factors. One of those was, of course, the emergence of other states: the claims of the one reinforced the claims of the other. Diplomacy or war might determine the outcome. State frontiers might not coincide with other frontiers, those of language and religion for example. The state might seek to ensure that they did. A principle of consolidation could become a principle of contest both within a state and among states. The emergence of the nation-state, in which the allegiance was to the state as a community, could only intensify that duality and the challenges it presented.

In colonial territories, Europeans would try to apply some of the principles with which they had become familiar in Europe. They had, as in Europe, another inducement to do so, their own rivalries. If, moreover, they did not settle disputes among themselves in the colonies, their relations in Europe might worsen. They settled such disputes in the colonies – between Britain and the Netherlands, Britain and France, Britain and Spain – often with more reference to their own convenience than to the conditions of the territories in actual or potential dispute.

The colonial frontiers, moreover, were sometimes no more than lines on a map. They were often designed to avoid future disputes rather than resolve present conflicts. Often, too, they went beyond any effective colonial rule. One principle of the frontier – that it was between states – might prevail over another – that it determined the allegiance of those behind it. That sometimes came second, rather than first.

That mattered less, perhaps, while the frontiers were in fact those of colonial dependencies. They were, however, inherited by states in a world of nation-states. Nation-states require a more intense allegiance and a sense of community. Establishing them in Southeast Asia was likely, though in a different way, to be as difficult as in Europe, if not at times more so, since the frontiers had emerged as a part of a process of settlement among other states, not among the states directly concerned.

The regulation of frontiers among these states was not likely, as earlier in Europe, to be the subject of diplomacy; still less likely, however, was it to be the subject of war. If colonial powers had settled their frontiers with a view to avoiding war, the states that they thus created inherited the frontiers in the post-colonial phase. The world in that phase was dominated by the two super-powers of the period that followed the Second World War. Any change among other states, or indeed within them, was a subject of their jealous interest. It was a world not without any conflict, but it was one without major conflict: the tension of the Cold War between the super-powers intensified but it limited the conflict among others. The boundaries of the states were rarely changed, though battles might be fought across them. Too much was at stake. It was an apparent paradox, but not a real one, that in a world of states boundaries were more difficult to change than in a world of empires when bargains and deals had been relatively easy to make. The existence of international organisations looked the same way.

The tensions that followed the end of the Cold War phase point up the features of its predecessor. New states were formed out of the Soviet Union, their frontiers, those of the old republics, often under challenge. But other frontiers were also under pressure. Yugoslavia disintegrated. A war was fought in the Persian Gulf.

For most of the postwar period, however, governments and peoples had to accept the frontiers they inherited, illogical though they might be, ineffective though they might have been. Governments tended to act like the governments of nation-states, though nations did not necessarily exist. They were more active than colonial governments in providing services. They expected to unite and rule, not divide and rule. In Southeast Asia the results are still being worked out. The extent of national integration clearly varies. Undeniably, however, the sense of being, say, Indonesian or Malaysian has taken hold, and the sense of being, say, Thai or Vietnamese, has intensified. The position of other groups within the states – of the Kedazans in East Malaysia or of the Malayo-Muslims in Thailand – is problematical. But it may be argued that, for all their arbitrariness, the frontiers have been a major contribution to the stability of Southeast Asia in the contemporary period.

Without an explanation drawn from colonial and post-colonial history, it is difficult to explain the frontiers of modern Southeast Asia, so arbitrary do they seem. But they are less arbitrary on the mainland than they are in the archipelago. In the former they give a particular shape to states that had been assuming that shape in general over some centuries. The Burman, Thai, Vietnamese, and Khmer states are recognisable entities before the Europeans, disputing or avoiding disputes among themselves, determined their frontiers in international treaties, placed them on their maps and in due course marked some of those frontiers on the ground. In the archipelago the intervention of the Europeans, which took place over a longer period, often with greater intensity, was also more decisive in shaping the frontiers that their successors were to inherit as those of nation-states.

It was largely in the nineteenth and early twentieth centuries that the frontiers took their current shape. The role of the British, the leading European power in a world then led by the Europeans, was decisive. Their policy was not to take over Southeast Asia as they took over India. They resolved not to make China another India. Nor did they make an India of Further India. Burma, in fact, was the only substantial territory over which they assumed dominion – that indeed they did only in three phases – and it was also the only substantial state with which they clearly can be said to have gone to war. Britain's policy in Burma was exceptional. It was in a sense a British Indian policy determined more by a concern for the security of

British dominion in India than by the strategic and commercial interests that determined the policies of the British elsewhere in Southeast Asia.

For Britain in the world in general, it may be said, commercial and financial interests came first. It had other interests, particularly in India, where the establishment of its dominion antedated the advent of the industrial revolution. But, with its early advantage in industrialisation, its concerns were with the opportunities for trade: if that were free, it could benefit. Dominion was not desirable in itself: it was desirable only if there were no other way of providing for the stability of the countries with and in which the British traded and for the security of their homeland, their possessions, and their trade routes. Indeed it can be argued that the British looked towards a world of states, where, as in Europe, each was sovereign and theoretically equal, in which each related to the others by diplomacy rather than by dominion, by commerce rather than by conflict. 'It would be on the most selfish view of the case, far better for us that the people of India ... were ruled by their own kings, but wearing our broad cloth, and working with our cutlery, than that they were performing their salams to English collectors and English Magistrates, but were too ignorant to value, or too poor to buy English manufactures...'[3]

If that is the case in general, it is also the case in Southeast Asia, except in Burma, where the concern for the security of a unique dominion in India overlaid the more normal concerns of the British. The connexion with the Malay archipelago, Stamford Raffles wrote, 'stands on a very different footing from that with the people of India. However inviting and extensive their resources, it is considered that they can be best drawn forth by the native energies of the people themselves, uninfluenced by foreign rule, and unfettered by foreign regulations, and that it is by the reciprocal advantage of commerce, and commerce alone, that we may best promote our own interests and their advancement.'[4] Indeed the limited British interest in dominion helped to give Southeast Asia its peculiar political configuration in the nineteenth century and endow it with the often apparently illogical though enduring frontiers of the twentieth century. The British did not use the power of which they disposed to rule Southeast Asia. They used it to establish conditions which suited the variety of their interests, and reflected their acceptance of contingency and compromise. 'There is a moral frugality which is at the root of all pecuniary frugality; and no nation which is lavish of pledges and promises which it may be unable to redeem, can have any grasp at all of the first principle of a true State economy.'[5]

In the nineteenth century, indeed, it seems that Southeast Asia was less important to the British for its own sake than it was for the sake of their extraneous interests. Burma was important to them for the sake of India. The Straits Settlements were important to them because of their need to provide for the security of the route to China. Borneo, too, derived what importance it had from its position in regard to that route. The policy the British adopted towards the other colonial powers in Southeast Asia reflected the importance of their relationships with them in Europe. Only in the twentieth century – with the advent of rubber and the motor car and the need for dollars – did Malaya assume major importance for Britain on economic grounds. Singapore also assumed a new importance as a naval base, designed to permit a one-ocean fleet to fulfil the needs of a two-ocean empire. But that was in the days of Britain's relative decline. Intrinsically Southeast Asia was more important to Britain then than in the days of its primacy.

These views, those of the authorities in India and in Great Britain, were not always those of the local authorities, or of British merchants and adventurers in the region. At times, indeed, they were at odds. Given the slow communications of the period, particularly before the opening of the telegraph in 1871, it was possible for initiatives at the local level to pre-empt imperial policy, even to defy it. 'My instructions were simple', wrote Sir Andrew Clarke about the intervention in Malaya in 1874. 'The Colonial Office was thoroughly dissatisfied with the state of affairs in the Peninsula. I was to make it the subject of careful enquiry, and report my views as soon as possible. I fear that in some quarters there lurks a belief in the efficacy of reports... It was necessary to act in the first place and to report afterwards...'[6]

It was also possible for the inventive to interpret imperial policy in a more expansive direction than it was intended, even to stand it on its head. Were those whom vessels of the British Navy attacked on Sir James Brooke's advice pirates or not? His critics thought not: 'our venerated patriot', Cobden gloated, 'was almost as savagely assaulted as the Bornean Dyaks themselves – the difference being in the weapons employed rather than in the spirit of the attack...'[7] Even members of the government were doubtful: the Raja wanted 'a squadron kept up to repress Bornean piracy on the same principle that we keep one up on the African Coast to put down the slave trade'. He was apt 'to imagine English ships and troops may be used for the promotion of civilisation and commerce generally, by the pulling down of unfriendly and the setting-up of friendly chiefs'. Lord Stanley, Under-Secretary at the Foreign Office, was 'not clear that we have a right, or that it is expedient, to carry interference so far'.[8] Central restraint was mingled with local adventure. The overall outcome might be a mixed one, one, moreover, that might puzzle other powers, princes and peoples.

Even the acquisition of territory in Burma was arguably a second best policy. The British had made contact with the Burman monarchy as a result, not so much of commercial interests, as of territorial ones. The establishment of British dominion in Bengal coincided with the establishment of Burman dominion in Arakan. That frontier was difficult to establish, difficult for both sides to accept and enforce, and the problem was repeated in respect of Assam and Manipur. The frontiers were the more difficult to establish, accept and enforce because the attitudes of the two powers differed. Their political dynamics clashed. A Burman monarch had universalist claims. The new British dominion in India could not accept challenge from an Asian power on the sub-continent or in its immediate neighbourhood. Dealing with Burma on the basis of equality was difficult to conceive, given that the Burmans did not accept that such a dealing could be accompanied by an effective recognition of a difference in power and indeed often had to be. At times the British in India believed that they must try to fit Burma into the sub-continental pattern of subsidiary alliance, as Francklin suggested to Wellesley.[9] At the very least Burma must de facto recognise Britain's supremacy. Witnessing the first only made it more difficult for the Burmans to accept the second. War was the outcome. A decisive victory would demonstrate Britain's power and thus produce a more compliant view. The aim was not to acquire territory, but 'to produce such an impression of the power and resources of the British Empire in India as will deter the Court of Ava from any attempt again to disturb the friendly relations which may be re-established by the result of the present contest'.[10] A decisive victory evaded Governor-General Lord Amherst. Taking Arakan and Tenasserim was an alternative way to mark Britain's supremacy.

The policy did not work. Defeating Burma and depriving it of territory did not lead to friendship but to resentment. The defeated Burman monarch found it difficult to accept even the patient Henry Burney as Resident, and his successor wanted to disregard the Treaty of Yandabo: he declared that he would have nothing to say to the treaties, 'that they had not been made by him, and that we had never conquered him'.[11] A second war arose out of commercial disputes at Rangoon. But defending the somewhat disreputable mercantile interests involved was not Governor-General Lord Dalhousie's main purpose. Once the crisis had begun – and the combustible Commodore Lambert did nothing to damp it down – it had to be carried through. 'We can't afford to be shown to the door anywhere in the East.'[12] Victory was again marked by acquisition of territory. Dalhousie believed that a treaty could not usefully be secured.

The remnant kingdom had some chance of survival under Mindon Min, who sought to nurture its independence without alienating the British. But in his latter years the balance became more difficult to sustain, and his successor failed in the task. The approach of the French, based in northern Vietnam, narrowed Burma's chances. According to François Deloncle, the French leader, Jules Ferry, asked him to negotiate a supplementary agreement with Burma in 1884

> in such a way that the British might become aware of our desire to develop an interest in independent upper Burma, where they were so jealous of their own influence, and that, thenceforth, they might be

prepared to make exchanges which would allow us, if need be, against the withdrawal of our interest in Burma, to obtain concessions in Siam. This would at least enable us to keep the British on tenderhooks in the Malay Peninsula. What Jules Ferry wanted was to conclude an agreement with Burma which would give him the tiller in Siam.[13]

What his policy prompted was the third Burma war. It ended in annexation. The frontier of Burma had to be settled with a European power.

The French had been Britain's main European rivals in India and had conceived their eighteenth-century venture in Vietnam as a way of getting even. The renewal of the venture in the nineteenth century was not, however, opposed by the British. They had attempted to develop what they saw as normal relations with Vietnam, but their missions had been rejected by Minh-mang and his successors. They were disposed to conclude that the French would not damage, and might indeed promote, the interests of commerce: 'a second Cherbourg in the East' was not 'cause for serious anxiety'.[14] It was important, however, that, if France established a dominion in Vietnam, it should not extend into Siam and Laos, thus threatening the security of British interests in Burma and the Malay Peninsula. The crisis came with the crisis between France and Siam in 1893. Britain did not back Siam as much as its king hoped it would: Rosebery's policy was to persuade the Thais to submit to French demands before they asked for more.[15] But some limits were placed on the French by the Anglo-French agreement of 1896. The improvement in Anglo-French relations, promoted by apprehension about the Germans, led to further agreements. Siam's boundaries in Cambodia were adjusted. In 1909 it also transferred to Britain its claims over the northern Malay states. That established the frontier of the future Malaya, but it left Malayo-Muslims in Pattani on the Thai side of the frontier. That decision, however, reflected the pattern that Anglo-Malay-Thai relations had assumed during the nineteenth century.

Britain's interest in the peninsula had focused since the late eighteenth century on the Straits Settlements, Penang, Melaka, Singapore. Strategically they guarded the route to China; commercially they tended to look outward to the archipelago and beyond rather than inward to the peninsula. The development of tin mining in Perak and Selangor began to interest them more in the peninsula itself. Only with rubber did these economic interests acquire an imperial importance. The strategic importance of the settlements had, however, made the imperial government anxious to exclude other powers from the peninsula, and the local interests had continued to build relatively informal connexions with Malay rulers that were to serve as the epitome of the Anglo-Malay relationship when it was formalised after 1874.

The policy of excluding other powers from the peninsula led indeed towards the making of one of the most novel frontiers in nineteenth-century

Southeast Asia. The Anglo-Dutch Treaty of 1824 was designed to settle current and avoid future disputes between the two European powers. Britain had held Penang since 1786 and, guided by Stamford Raffles, had secured Singapore in 1819. If it also were to acquire Melaka from the Dutch, it would have three settlements along the straits, and their security would be increased if the Dutch, who had claims over Perak and Johor, abstained from intervening on the peninsula in the future. At the same time, the British would leave their old settlement at Benkulen in west Sumatra, and cut off their political connexions with rulers on that island. A kind of line was thus drawn on the map, though it was not made explicit lest it provoke other powers to challenge the way when the British and the Dutch were dividing the region between them. 'The situation in which we and the Dutch stand to each other is part only of our difficulty. That in which we both stand to the rest of the world as exclusive Lords of the East is one more reason for terminating our relative difficulties as soon as we can.'[16] It was not yet a line between two empires: it was a line beyond which two empires should not extend. Over the subsequent decades it became a frontier. But even in its initial form it was unprecedented. Peninsula and archipelago had enjoyed a common past. States – Aceh, Johore, the Portuguese, the Dutch – had previously had a footing on both sides of the straits. Now the straits had become a kind of frontier. In Southeast Asia the sea unites; the Europeans used it to divide.

The settlement did not go unchallenged in subsequent years. There were disputes between the British and the Dutch, particularly in the 1830s and 1840s. Irritated by the restrictive commercial policies of the Dutch, the British were tempted to challenge their territorial extension. The treaty gave them little scope in Sumatra, however, and in the 1850s and 1860s Dutch extension came once more to seem acceptable. Economically the Dutch became more liberal, and the advent of other powers suggested the need to avoid renewed Anglo-Dutch dispute. 'With a decent trade tariff we can keep all enemies from Europe out of the East Indies';[17] 'a liberal trade policy in our possessions will constitute an essential contribution to the defence of our territory against a foreign enemy.'[18] The questions that Sumatra had raised the convention of 1871 was intended to settle. In fact, it precipitated a long struggle between Aceh and the Dutch. In Sumatra the British, however, did not go back on their policy of accepting Dutch predominance in the archipelago. 'Pot-valiant Holland sailed in to find a wasps' nest. For the Achinese have proved stubborn fighters, and take considerable delight in terminating the existence of those unfortunates whom their trusty ally the malaria leaves alive... The natural conceit of the Dutchman forbids his giving in...'[19]

In North Borneo the British had gone back on their policy of accepting Dutch predominance in the 1840s, and as a result another frontier was established. The enterprise had been initiated by a British adventurer, James Brooke, who believed, like Raffles, that the policy was a mistake. The Dutch had 'gradually and effectually destroyed all rightful authority...their doubtful title and oppressive tenure would...render the downfall of their rule in the Archipelago, certain and easy, before the establishment of a liberal Government and conciliatory policy'.[20] He secured some backing from the British government, then in dispute with the Dutch, and anxious to secure openings for British commerce. It did not take over the raj in Sarawak that he had secured from the sultan of Brunei. It did, however, accept, also from Brunei, the grant of the island of Labuan, which became a colony in 1848. In 1847 it made a treaty with the sultan, binding him not to make cessions to other powers without Britain's consent. Again this kept the Dutch, and others, out, without making the territory British. It was only reluctantly that the British took further steps. In 1888 they established protectorates over Sarawak, by then considerably expanded at Brunei's expense; over the remnant of the sultanate; and over North Borneo, a state secured by cession and lease from the sultanate and from Sulu and ruled by the British North Borneo Chartered Company. With the establishment of the protectorates, Britain proceeded to settle their frontiers with the Dutch territory in Borneo.

The creation of frontiers did not mean the creation of states. In the colonial world that was not in any case intended. But states emerged with the end of the colonial world, and the post-colonial states inherited those frontiers. The 'stretch' of Indonesia, with 'its hybrid pseudo-Hellenic name', does not 'remotely correspond to any precolonial domain', as Benedict Anderson puts it: 'at least until General Suharto's brutal invasion of ex-Portuguese East Timor in 1975, its boundaries have been those left behind by the last Dutch conquests (c. 1910).'[21] Moreover, the post-colonial states saw themselves generally as nation-states and the frontiers as those of nation-states. The established frontiers thus had a somewhat different purpose and a wholly different rationale.

Drawing those frontiers had been undertaken to avoid dispute. Power, interest and expediency had been at work. There was no necessary coincidence between such frontiers and the divisions created by language, community, religion, or 'ethnicity'. That did not make the task nation-states set themselves any easier. At the same time it has to be said that drawing frontiers that did coincide with the divisions of language, community, religion, or ethnicity would have been a far from easy task, if not an impossible one. The arbitrary legacy of the colonial past was no more disruptive than a redrawing of frontiers would have been. Almost surely it was less.

The process is yet incomplete and may be seen, as Edward Said points out, in another light. 'Along with authorized figures – the ruler, the national heroes and martyrs, the established religious authorities – the newly triumphant politicians seem to require borders and passports first of all. What had once been the imaginative liberation of a people...and the audacious metaphoric charting of spiritual territory usurped by colonial masters were quickly translated into and accommodated by a world system of barriers, maps, frontiers, police forces, customs and exchange controls.'[22] In Africa the people cross and defy the borders the rulers erect. Much less do they do so in Southeast Asia. The states themselves are more effective in regulating movement. But some of it certainly escapes them, particularly as the supply of labour in one country adjusts to the demand in another. The states themselves seek to channel that too, for example by developing 'growth triangles', associating the differing interests of the states in geographical proximity with those of global investors and entrepreneurs.   ●

---

1   Hermann v. Helmholtz, quoted R. Hofstadter and W. P. Metzger, *The Development of Academic Freedom in the United States*, New York and London: Columbia University Press, 1955, p. 389.

2   C. A. Fisher, in W. G. East and O. H. K. Spate, eds, *The Changing Map of Asia*, London: Methuen, 1950, p. 197.

3   Macaulay, quoted G. Bennett, ed., *The Concept of Empire*, London: Black, pp. 72–3.

4   Raffles' Minute on Malay College. quoted H. E. Egerton, *Sir Stamford Raffles*, London: Unwin, 1900, p. 228.

5   *The Economist*, XVI, No. 797, 4 December 1858.

6   quoted W. D. McIntyre, *The Imperial Frontier in the Tropics, 1865–75*, London and New York: Macmillan, 1967, p. 209.

7   Cobden/Sturge, 16/10/1852. Add MS 43656, p. 309, British Museum.

8   Memorandum, 2/8/1852. FO 12/11, Public Record Office, London.

9   D. G. E. Hall, *Europe and Burma*, London: Oxford University Press, 1945, p. 94.

10   quoted G. P. Ramachandra, 'Anglo-Burmese Relations, 1795–1826', PhD thesis, University of Hull, 1977, p. 391.

11   quoted W. S. Desai, *History of the British Residency in Burma*, Rangoon: University of Rangoon, 1939, p. 297.

12   quoted D. G. E. Hall, ed., *The Dalhousie–Phayre Correspondence*, London: Oxford University Press, 1932, p. xix.

13   quoted P. Tuck, *The French Threat to Siamese Independence 1858–1907*, Bangkok and Cheney: White Lotus, 1995, p. 72.

14   quoted B. L. Evans, 'The attitudes and policies of Great Britain and China towards French expansion in Cochin China, Cambodia, Annam and Tongking 1858–83', PhD thesis, University of London, 1961, p. 41.

15   J. Chandran, *The Contest for Siam*, Kuala Lumpur: Oxford University Press, 1977, pp. 72–3.

16   Memorandum, 15/1/1824, with Mr Canning's notes. Dutch Records, I/2/31, India Office Library.

17   van Bosse/London, 12/3/69. quoted M. Kuitenbrouwer, *The Netherlands and the Rise of Modern Imperialism*, New York, Oxford: Berg, 1991, pp. 58–9.

18   E. De Waal, Dutch Colonial Minister, 1871 quoted in G. J. A. Raven and N. A. M. Rodger, *Navies and Armies*, Edinburgh: Donald, 1990, p. 59.

19   Guy Boothby, *On the Wallaby or Through the East and Across Australia*, London: Longmans, 1894, p. 80.

20   quoted N. Tarling, *The Burthen, the Risk, and the Glory*, Kuala Lumpur: Oxford University Press, 1982, p. 20.

21   B. Anderson, *Imagined Communities*, London and New York: Verso, 1991, p. 120.

22   E. Said, *Culture and Imperialism*, New York: Knopf, 1993, p. 307.

COLONIAL AUTHORITY

Writers on the history of empire in general, or on the history of the British empire in particular, have rarely pulled Southeast Asia into focus. The perceptions they have developed in studying other areas may yet be useful in interpreting the history of Southeast Asia. At the same time, the Southeast Asian experience may test out their theories, and offer the possibility of refining or amplifying them.

Robinson and Gallagher studied the 'imperialism of free trade' and then moved on to Africa and the Victorians. Though he published no major work of his own, John Gallagher's further conclusions were published post-humously in *The Decline, Revival and Fall of the British Empire*.[1] All the works reflected on the nature of the relationship between imperial rulers and peoples who were ruled. The key relationship, they argued, was that with the local elite. Empire could not exist without securing its cooperation. The history of empire was a series of versions of that collaboration.[2]

Robinson and Gallagher admitted that their theories on the imperialism of free trade were affected by the position in which Britain found itself when they were writing in the late 1940s and 1950s. They were apprehensive of 'the colonial possibilities of the Marshall plan':[3] the US had established ways of collaborating with the Western European powers that, by economic and other means, directed their course without requiring overt political control. Like most of the best historians, Robinson and Gallagher not only looked at new material; they also looked at old material with new eyes. Each age constructs a view of the past, and historians are not exempt from the process. Their task is rather to re-position the past in relation to the present. It is likely that they will offer a perception that echoes some concern of the present. But it may also cast an additional light on the past, recovering some insight that had been lost, re-establishing some connexion across the generations or across the centuries, so as to advance a fuller understanding of the human condition.

Gallagher's theories on the elite, and on imperial relationships with the elite, also reflected concerns that came to mind as empire ended. The British were withdrawing from their formal political and constitutional links with colonial and dependent territories. Yet they still hoped to continue useful connexions with them. They looked for stability. They hoped to be on good terms or to get on to good terms with the new leaders. In the context of such thinking, it was natural for historians to look at the connexions that had earlier existed between independent states and the British. But even with respect to the dependent territories it was recognised that the ties had not been, and indeed could not have been, merely military, political and constitutional. Colonial regimes had relied in substantial measure on other factors: the compliance of the ruled; their isolation from other powers; their lack of a sense of nationalism. It was also important that the regimes did not attempt to do too much. Active governments, even those that were well-meaning, were more likely to provoke opposition than those the objectives of which were limited, as the experience of the Ethical Policy in Netherlands India suggested.

In some respects, indeed, there is a continuity among the pre-colonial, colonial, and post-colonial regimes. No regime, colonial or otherwise, can after all exist without an elite group that, in some way or ways, ties the mass of the people to the state. In pre-colonial Southeast Asia, as elsewhere, such ties might take bureaucratic or patrimonial forms, or both. Each has its advantages and its drawbacks. A bureaucratic state may come to exist almost for the sake of the bureaucracy rather than the state: the elite becomes alienated from the people and is itself difficult to control. It may also be penetrated by obligations to the family that add to its corruptibility. Familial obligations may, of course, be in themselves another way of binding a state together. The ruler is the head of a family which imposes obligations on the ruler and the ruled. But that very extended family contains within it families much less extended, the obligations of which, no less intense, may not coincide. In much of Southeast Asia, for most of its history underpopulated, personal ties were more important than any other. The binding of followers to a leader, though also of a leader to his followers, was the most significant of social-political patterns. More rarely, states adopted a more bureaucratic approach. The prime example was Vietnam: there indeed bureaucracy and familial ties contended. 'Cliques inevitably issue primarily from the father-son and elder brother-younger brother relationship and later spread to other men', Minh-mang noted in 1839.[4]

Colonial authority could not rely merely on force. Of that it had too little, and when it was deployed it had to be deployed decisively. A drawn-out conflict it was desirable to avoid: an impression of invulnerability was essential. Colonial authority had also therefore to rely upon an elite. That it could not supply on its own. Colonial regimes, aside from the colonies of settlement, rarely had large numbers of Europeans at their disposal. They were bound to use indigenous elites, whose support had to be secured and retained. In some sense they were bound to pursue the bureaucratic model, since they could not in general rely on a network of familial or pseudo-familial obligations. In practice they tended to pursue a mix of the models. At the higher level, they might rely on a bureaucracy, staffed more or less by Europeans. Otherwise they might rely on an indigenous elite, which might be partially bureaucratised, but would depend on an extensive network of obligations for survival and acceptance. Only by winning the support of such an elite could a colonial power hope to survive. In turn that elite could only be of help to the colonial power, or to itself, if it had the capacity to win the support of the mass of the people. 'In order to attain good feelings', Governor Goedhart wrote in 1928, 'it is first of all necessary that we remember that our power in Aceh, aside from the force of arms, depends in the main on the *uleebalangs* (local chiefs). Through them and with them we can win over the people. Without them in the long run we will accomplish nothing in Aceh.'[5] Where colonial regimes used force, it was designed to sustain such a system, not to replace it.

The mix of models was essential, but it was bound to be defective. If the elite were identified with the colonial power, they would be less able to win the support of the masses. Indeed the system might be oppressive and alienating. That was true of Java, as the cultivation system was introduced. The Resident of Rembang believed that 'the corruption and abuse of power by the native chiefs are so deeply rooted, and the whole system upon which European power in these lands is exercised offers them so many opportunities to commit more or less serious offences without penalty, that it is almost impossible to tear the evil out, root and branch, all at once'.[6] Bureaucratic and familial models might clash as they had in the pre-colonial phase, but in new ways.

Over time, therefore, the relationship was likely to change. But it would be difficult for the colonial regime to respond by changing the pattern. A new elite might emerge. But winning its support would be difficult to achieve unless the existing elite were cast aside. Such a change a colonial government might fear to undertake. Could it risk rejecting old collaborators in pursuit of new? Or was it better to stick with the tried and relatively true? Which devil should the foreign devil choose, the one it knew, the one it did not know? The Spaniards did not follow the advice of Sinibaldo de Mas.

In part the answer also depended on the nature of the new elite and its objectives. Its emergence was likely to owe something to the modernisation of colonial society through the operation of economic forces and to the provision by government or other agencies of education as an aid to general efficiency but also as an avenue of personal advancement. A colonial state could hardly avoid these events. It might survive to the extent that it could come to terms with them. A moderate elite, willing to work with rather than overthrow the colonial power, might offer the colonial ruler novel opportunities, if it could realise them. They would probably not be long-term. The new relationship, if achieved, might only be an interim deal, a step on the way to a political independence that would put the colonial power and the new elite on yet a different footing, establishing quite a different pattern of collaboration. In any case, the elite might be divided. Moderates might form only a part of it. They would be under challenge and their failure – and the failure of their collaboration – might mean that they would be cast aside.

Securing the compliance of the ruled had an external as well as internal aspect: it was in some sense an international or intercolonial matter. If the ruled could not look for support or help from outside, they were less able to contemplate overthrowing their rulers. In the earlier centuries of European contact with Southeast Asia, intercolonial rivalries had been apparent, and at times Asian rulers had tried to turn them to account. But, though the colonial regimes began in rivalry, their consolidation brought out what they had in common. The British wanted the Dutch to prevail on the archipelago, as the treaty of 1824 indicated. This meant that Indonesian states and Indonesian peoples had little hope of securing support against the Dutch and the policy was re-affirmed in the treaty of 1871: the Sultan of Aceh could secure no help from the British when war broke out with the Dutch in 1873. American intervention in the Philippines in effect recruited the US to the rank of colonial powers. In 1912 the Dutch afforded the Japanese most-favoured-nation treatment in commerce, hoping to defer their political ambitions. After the First World War the British became deeply apprehensive of international Communism. Perhaps their fears were not exaggerated. It offered an internal threat they might cope with. But it also offered a cross-frontier challenge to the colonial powers, breaching the de facto agreement that the Europeans stood together, and advocated that non-Europeans stood together against them. That would be a more intractable problem.

Risings against the colonial powers had been limited, not only in local, but also in international support. The Filipino revolutionaries of the 1890s, unlike the Southeast Asian nationalists after the Second World War, were on their own. All they could secure was half-hearted support from the Japanese when they were fighting the Spaniards; they secured no support when they had to fight the Americans. Insulation was an effective means of sustaining colonial rule. Colonial powers extended such insulation by censorship – as in the nineteenth-century Philippines – and by police intelligence – as in the Singapore of the 1920s and early 1930s. Pre-empting Communist subversion was seen to be a common enterprise. Was the movement 'headed up in one place' the American Governor-General wondered?[7] Secretary of State Stimson had already agreed on collaboration with the Recherche in Netherlands India. French authorities 'assisted the British police in Singapore'.[8]

Ideas nevertheless penetrated, including the nationalist ideas common in nineteenth-century Europe. They were to appeal to new elites and make them less accommodating. 'We have put the wine of Western democratic ideas into the old bottles of the East and there is a terrible ferment going on,' Austen Chamberlain wrote in 1917.[9] Nationalism also affected the military equation. Colonial powers were not able entirely to rely on military forces from their homeland: they were insufficient; but most of them were able to mobilise forces from their colonial territories. Arming the majority people was dangerous, they recognised, and the Indian Mutiny bore this out. But arming minorities, rather than majorities, might be safe, even advantageous. Colonial powers tended to look to minority groups, and to concentrate on particular peoples or areas from which they might draw loyal support. The British identified 'military races' in India; they used non-Burmans in Burma. They were cautious about using Malays in Malaya.[10] The Spaniards recruited from Pampanga, and the KNIL (the Dutch colonial army) often looked to Maluku, Ambonese, Menadonese, Timorese, 'warlike races', by contrast to the Javanese for whom 'entering the ranks was the equivalent of a social misfortune'.[11]

The rise of nationalism would defeat such a policy, as Sir John Seeley recognised, by uniting the peoples concerned.

> We could subdue the mutiny of 1857, formidable as it was, because it spread through only a part of the army, because the people did not actively sympathise with it, and because it was possible to find native Indian races who would fight on our side. But the moment a mutiny is but threatened, which shall be no mere mutiny, but the expression of a universal feeling of nationality, at that moment all hope is at an end, as all desire ought to be at an end, of preserving our [Indian] Empire.[12]

In the meantime, however, colonial powers could raise armies for their main purpose, that of establishing and maintaining peace and order within their territories. Such forces were in fact armed constabularies, and indeed so described in the American Philippines. Their usefulness in defending the country against outside attack would be limited, since they had no national identification with their ruler, nor indeed with the majority of the ruled. The defence of the realm would depend on the metropolitan army, even more on its navy. The main aim was to fend off rival predators. The stability of the nineteenth century largely depended on the British navy.

Nationalists recognised the strengths and weaknesses in colonial rule. It might be hard to acquire arms and to fight battles, but it might not be essential to do so. The creation of a sense of unity might suffice. Sometimes the nationalists seem hopelessly at sea, and their purposes obscure. What was Rizal's purpose when he organised the Liga Filipina? Why did Sukarno put so much emphasis on playing down the differences among nationalists, Communists, and Muslims? 'What is Sukarno? A nationalist? An Islamist? A Marxist! Readers, Sukarno is a mixture of all these isms.'[13] The idea was to confront the colonial regimes. If they depended so much on disunity among those they ruled, unity might make them change their course, even make their position impossible.

One problem was, of course, to extend that unity by acquiring mass support. The colonial regimes depended on those they coopted to retain mass compliance or avoid mass opposition. Disrupting that link would thus be important. The development of colonial rule and the impact of economic forces performed some of the task. For one of the most important features of colonial government, and one further reason for its longevity, was that it had a limited purpose. Its scope was narrow: it aimed to maintain a sufficient measure of law and order and to extract, directly or indirectly, a substantial measure of profit. Otherwise it was relatively inactive for most of its history. That indeed made it possible to rely on a traditional elite. And it made it easier for that elite to retain the allegiance of a largely peasant population, since traditional patterns were not entirely disrupted. While this was so, moreover, the extent to which alien rule was so perceived was also limited. Those who were ruled had little direct impact contact with European administrators.

It was when European rule became more active that it became more alienating. Rather paradoxically, that was often when it became more well-meaning. The Ethical Policy of the Dutch brought their administration into closer contact with the village, and the peasants felt they were being pressed by alien forces to do alien things, albeit in their rulers' view for their own good. Modernisation made it difficult to secure continued loyalty from the elite. But it also dislodged the traditional allegiance of the masses.

Colonial authority in the nineteenth-century sense could not endure. The imperial powers were themselves adopting policies that, adding to the impact of economic forces, undermined it. Old elites lost, if not their traditional attitude, their traditional influence. New elites aspired to replace both them and their colonial rulers. The masses, freed from older ties, were open to mobilisation. Stepping up the activities of police and intelligence services would delay and impede the changes, but not stop them. The intervention of other powers, so far avoided or contained, would be crucial, both to the pace of change and to the configuration of the outcome.

The old colonial authority would modify the relationships upon which it relied, but that would not necessarily involve their displacement. The new elite, securing power within the former colonial territories, had still to work out its relationships with the former colonial power, and also the other states with which it now came into direct contact. Would those relationships be cast in a neo-colonial mould? Within each territory, the elite had to secure the support or the confidence of the masses. How far would they rely on the devices of the colonial powers and their security regimes?   ●

1   J. Gallagher, *The Decline, Revival and Fall of the British Empire*, Cambridge: Cambridge University Press, 1983.
2   Cf R. Robinson, 'Non-European Foundations of European Imperialism: Sketch for a Theory of Collaboration', in Roger Owen and Bob Sutcliffe, eds, *Studies in the Theory of Imperialism*, London: Longman, 1972, pp. 118–40.
3   Cf R. Robinson, in F. Madden and D. K. Fieldhouse, *Oxford and the Idea of Commonwealth*, London: Croom Helm, 1982, pp. 45, 47.
4   quoted Woodside, *Vietnam and the Chinese Model*, Cambridge, Mass.: Harvard University Press, 1971, p. 38.
5   quoted Eric Morris, 'Aceh: Social Revolution and the Islamic Vision', in Audrey Kahin, ed., *Regional Dynamics of the Indonesian Revolution*, Honolulu: University of Hawaii Press, 1985, p. 85.
6   quoted R. Elson, *Village Java under the Cultivation System, 1830–1870*, Sydney: Allen & Unwin, 1994, p. 125.
7   quoted T. Friend, *The Blue-Eyed Enemy*, Princeton University Press, 1988, p. 46.
8   Laurent Metzger, 'Joseph Ducroux, a French agent of the Comintern in Singapore (1931–1932)', *Journal of the Malaysian Branch Royal Asiatic Society*, 69.1 (June 1996), p. 5.
9   *The Austen Chamberlain Diary Letters*, ed. Robert C. Self, London: Royal Historical Society, 1995, p. 46.
10   Cf Nadzan Harun, 'British Defence Policy in Malaya, 1874–1918', in K. M. de Silva, et al, eds, *Asian Panorama*, New Delhi: Vikas, 1990, pp. 442–4
11   Gerke Teitler, *The Dutch Colonial Army in Transition*, Townsville: James Cook University, 1981, p. 4.
12   quoted Bennett, ed., *The Concept of Empire*, London: Black, p. 279.
13   quoted J. D. Legge, *Sukarno*, London: Lane, 1972, p. 142.

THE INDUSTRIAL REVOLUTION

Nineteenth-century Southeast Asia was affected not only by the political decisions of the Europeans but by the impact of the industrial revolution they brought to the world. Economic change in the nineteenth century and after indeed affected various parts of Southeast Asia in different ways not only because of their differing resources and their differing potential, but also because they were placed under different regimes. Those regimes adopted policies that affected the relationship between the development of the territories they ruled or aspired to rule and the economies of other parts of the world. Would their industries be undermined by competition? Would they produce food and raw materials for other countries? Would their economies become more export-oriented? If so, would they be more dependent on one or two commodities? These issues would be determined by political as well as economic decisions, by particular circumstances as well as general.

It is easy to antedate the development of the economic relationships that the industrial revolution brought about. Before the nineteenth century the trade between Europe and Asia had not, for the most part, been reciprocal in character. Pre-industrial Europe sought goods from Asia, but there was little that Asia wanted in return. The Portuguese and the Dutch made themselves traders within Asia, remitting the proceeds of their enterprise in the form of the spices that Europeans then sought. At first unable to compete in this venture, the English tried, on the whole vainly, to find a market for their manufactures in Asia. Their ability to compete improved in the late seventeenth and eighteenth centuries, with the emergence of new demands on Asia that they were better able and better placed to meet, for Indian textiles, for China tea. But they were in no position to develop a reciprocal trade. To pay for tea from China they transported to Canton opium from India and jungle and marine produce from Southeast Asia. The alternative was the precious metals upon which Spain relied.

This pattern was slow to disappear. The 1870s may mark a turning-point. Great Britain had been the first industrial state. Now, in Europe and in the US, industrialisation both spread and intensified. Bismarck's political unification of Germany gave an impulse to the spread of industry there: it struck down many obstacles to entrepreneurship; and at the end of the decade the state offered protection to over-expanded industries as they faced depression. The pace of change in Germany was comparable only to that in the US. There the end of the Civil War was followed by major attempts to develop and to industrialise, and in the US, as in Germany, the state was not unwilling to protect industry, as the McKinley tariff of 1891 was to show. Industrialisation affected other countries, too, though less strikingly. The state, but also individual entrepreneurs, were heavily involved in Russian industrialisation in the 1880s and 1890s. Britain lost the advantage of being first, though gaining opportunities for investment overseas and in the modernisation of other economies.

If the world was transforming itself, it was also brought closer together. Much of the early impulse to industrialisation, and of the government involvement in it, was infrastructural. Communications were dramatically improved, not only within countries, above all with railway-building, but among them. The most striking development in this respect was the opening of the Suez Canal in 1869. A French endeavour, it became important for the British, and indeed for all those in the West with interests in the East. But other ties were also developed about the same time. The electric telegraph reached Singapore in 1871 and linked Southeast Asia to Europe, China, and Australia during these years.

These two developments, taken together, were bound to affect the economic relationship of Asia with the outside world, and the position of Southeast Asian countries within that relationship. The inroads of Western manufactures on the India and China markets were not always as great as the manufacturers hoped. But there was a major shift towards the production in Asia of food and raw materials for markets in the industrialising West. That involved Asian countries, and areas in Asian countries, differentially. In general, it enhanced their dependence on exporting a limited number of crops with markets overseas, either as a result of their cheapness, or as a result of their special quality.

Trade within Asia did not, of course, disappear, but it changed its character. Previously, it had focused on the export of Indian textiles and of Indian drugs to other parts of Asia, on the importation into China of jungle and marine products and precious metals, on the export of manufactures from China. Such activities were not at once displaced, but they were put into the background. The new emphasis on an import-export relationship with the rest of the world was accompanied by a largely supportive regional differentiation. While, for example, tin and rubber were exported from Malaya, rice was taken to Malaya from Burma, Siam and Indo-China.

Even before 1870, a mixed pattern had been emerging. The merchants in Penang, and even in early Singapore, were still concerned with the 'country trade', with textiles, opium and goods for China. Those established in Java after the British conquest of 1811 still retained close ties to India, but they were also distributing British textiles. The disputes over the Anglo-Dutch treaty of 1824 related to duties charged upon goods from Europe as well as goods from other parts of Asia.

The same overlaying of patterns is apparent in the Philippines. More or less open to foreign trade before, Manila was explicitly opened in 1834, and other ports were to follow in 1855. Initially the trade was in rice taken to China. Then new opportunities opened up for sugar in Luzon and the Visayas, taken to Australia and to Europe, and for hemp produced in the Bikol region, taken to the US. In time, the Philippines became an importer of rice.

The intervention of governments was one of the factors in creating the mixed pattern of trade; the demands of the Western market and its supply of capital formed another. It was the latter that were in a sense to prevail after 1870. But government interventions were particularly strong before 1870. Indeed they distorted the play of economic forces, and that was no doubt a reason for their retreat after 1870. But in some respects they inserted a post-1870 pattern into a pre-1870 situation.

In the Philippines the Spanish government failed to intervene effectively. Always concerned lest they lost the Philippines, as they had once lost Manila, to a combination of foreign attack and domestic insurrection, the Spaniards made some attempts to develop the islands. In particular they tried to link their possession more effectively with the rest of the world, instead of merely with Mexico, by opening up the route round the Cape of Good Hope. They also established a new company, and an Economic Society, designed to develop new resources in the Philippines. Those endeavours had limited success. More effective was the revenue-raising tobacco monopoly created by General Basco. But the loss of Mexico and the other major possessions in America in the early nineteenth century meant that the Philippines had to seek other means of ensuring its survival. The only way was to facilitate foreign trade, opening the way to economic initiatives that would prompt social and political change. Commercial opportunity might indeed appease the British, though it ran the risk of subverting Spanish authority in other ways.

The Dutch, by contrast, intervened in the economy of Java with determination and effect. Earlier they had had little success in adapting to the changing nature of the trade within Asia. Their system, built up in the seventeenth century and oriented to supplying Europe with spices, failed to take advantage of the opportunities offered by the eighteenth-century European demands for textiles and tea, even though they had a number of advantages, including bases in India as well as in Southeast Asia. After the French wars, such opportunities were no longer available. Nor, indeed, did the Netherlands economy dispose of the capital that might help the Dutch turn the colonies they regained from the British to advantage. Government intervened to mobilise Javanese labour under the cultivation system, and to organise trade to the Netherlands under the consignment system. The pattern was more of an old colonial one than a post-1870 one. Java was treated as an appendage of the Dutch economy, and with the surpluses it created Dutch infrastructure was built and industry made to flourish. But, despite the controverted application of the treaty of 1824, British merchants drew some advantage from the development of Java, and indeed adapted to the system so well that they came to oppose changes that would introduce competitors. 'British mercantile houses carrying on trade with Java', it was reported in 1868, 'have expressed their hope that no reduction may take place in the duties there, as at present they have a practical monopoly of the business, which notwithstanding the heavy taxes levied on it enables them to make very large profits.'[1]

Singapore was part of the old pattern and of the new. Its initial success in many ways showed that it belonged to the old, though 'Kota Baru', as it was long known to indigenous traders, provided new routes and new products.[2] It was but the latest in the series of entrepots for intra-Asian and Southeast Asian trade that had triumphed at the tip of the straits, and history seemed to be in Raffles' mind. It distributed Indian textiles and opium; it welcomed traders from China, from the archipelago, from Vietnam, from Siam; and it had the unfair advantage of revenue support from India. But it also distributed British goods, enjoying that same support. Other countries thus became familiar with them. 'Since Singapore has become a settlement chintzes from Europe have been used as bathing clouts, broadcloths as trousers, Bugis satins and the batek silks of Java as hats. People carry silk umbrellas in their hands and wear leather sandals, and talk fluently in English, Bengali and Tamil. If an Englishman addresses them in Malay they reply in English.'[3]

In some ways, indeed, Singapore prepared the way for others, for rivals or emulators, for new ports if not entrepots, for Bangkok, Saigon, Makasar. That, of course, was always a source of Singapore concern. Rivals would catch up, and the pioneer's advantage would be lost. In the event, despite all its concerns, Singapore kept ahead. It became itself a local port in regard to Malaya, while it retained its entrepot function, albeit in new services or new products. In more recent times, it was itself to industrialise.

The mainland states were affected by these changes more indirectly than directly. Before 1870, their governments made no attempts to emulate the Dutch. At most they opened up their territories to the play of economic forces. In Burma, that was the policy of the British, first in Arakan and Tenasserim, and then in Pegu, and in the remnant kingdom, the ruler, Mindon Min, as part of his policy of 'defensive modernisation', made commercial treaties with the British and, more riskily, with others. Siam responded to the British more positively. It made a commercial treaty in 1826, and in 1855 accepted a treaty along the lines of the 'unequal' treaty imposed upon China. Vietnam, by contrast, failed to respond to British commercial missions. As a result, the British believed that the French could well pursue the task of 'opening' the kingdom.

After 1870 all these territories were affected by economic change, becoming, however, not so much sources of raw materials or of food for world markets, as sources of rice for other parts of Southeast Asia as they produced food and raw materials for world markets. In some respects, it might be said that not only did Southeast Asia in political terms come within a largely colonial framework; it also responded as a whole to the economic pressures that intensified after 1870. What happened in one part of Southeast Asia, politically or economically, affected the others, politically and economically.

The mainland states certainly produced other goods, though rice was their main export. A second focus of world interest was, as in the archipelago, on mineral wealth: the tin of Malaya and of Bangka, the rubies of Burma, the coal of Borneo and Vietnam. Oil was also discovered, and exported, in Burma, in Borneo and Sumatra, later in Sarawak and Brunei.

By the early twentieth century, indeed, the industrial revolution had moved into a new phase, and exerted new demands. One feature was the emergence of the automobile industry. Not only was there a demand for oil, but also a demand for rubber. This could be grown on plantations as well as by smallholders. Different parts of Southeast Asia again responded in different ways. Rubber tended to be a plantation crop in Malaya and Vietnam, a smallholder crop in many parts of Netherlands India.

The transformation of the Southeast Asian economies was striking. With the growth of exports went a growth in infrastructure, an expansion of economic activity and educational provision. Even under the cultivation system, it is now clear, as a result of the research of Cees Fasseur, R. E. Elson and others, that the Javanese peasant responded more positively as well as more diversely than earlier critics of that system were able to recognise. But there were limits on these changes, and they were perhaps stronger in Java than elsewhere. Much of the wealth that was created helped to build up infrastructural and industrial capacity in the Netherlands. A somewhat similar situation obtained in other territories. Burman nationalists complained of British firms. To use Norman Owen's phrase, the Bikol region prospered but it did not progress.[4] The industrial revolution spread in Europe and in the US. But there was little industrialisation in colonial Southeast Asia.

The focus on oil as a source of energy at the same time put Southeast Asia into a new political context. Japan industrialised, but had no oil of its own. Its determination to avoid the dependence on the US that implied was to prompt it to disrupt colonial Southeast Asia. In turn its defeat was to open up new political opportunities in Southeast Asia. There were also new economic opportunities. Singapore industrialised. Malaysia and Thailand joined the ranks of the industrialising. Others would follow. ●

---

1   Ord to Colonial Office, 3 August 1868 FO37/487; CO 273/21 [10377], Public Record Office, London.

2   cf A. Van Der Kraan, 'Bali and Lombok in the World Economy', *RIMA*, 27, 1 & 2, Winter–Summer 1993, p. 95.

3   Abdullah bin Abdul Kadir, *The Hikayat Abdullah*, trans. A. H. Hill, Kuala Lumpur: Oxford University Press, 1970, p. 162.

4   N. Owen, *Prosperity without Progress: Manila Hemp and Material Life in the Colonial Philippines*, Berkeley: University of California Press, 1984.

PARLIAMENTARY GOVERNMENT AND SOUTHEAST ASIA

In writing international history, it is customary, as in the practice of international diplomacy, to refer to the country as the actor: Britain did this; the Dutch decided that. That is often, of course, only a shorthand. What was officially done or decided might indeed take that form but the deed or decision might be far more complex in origin. Within a state there are many levels of action and decision-making, and they are rarely unanimous in outcome or even coherent. A more sophisticated view of international relations indeed extends its historiography further still. The late Christopher Thorne was one who sought to give international relations a larger meaning and its historiography a larger task. International historians, he believed, had to 'pursue their enquiries into areas which are usually thought of as the domain of the sociologist or social-psychologist, say, or of the economic or intellectual historian'.[1]

A similar approach is clearly valid for imperial and colonial history, perhaps even more so. That there were several layers of decision-making is evident; that there was a whole range of relationships besides the official ones is evident also. Decision-making could indeed be inconsistent: governors on the spot might differ from their remote superiors; naval officers might be at odds with civilian governors; the courts might be at odds with the executive.[2] At home, too, there was a range of decision-makers. Colonial Office and Foreign Office might differ; Treasury and Colonial Office might differ. Opinion might also vary. Increasingly that variance was not simply among an elite – did Castlereagh differ from Canning? or Palmerston from Aberdeen? – but among the public. The differences between Gladstone and Disraeli seemed more fundamental than those of their predecessors, more than they really were, partly because more public. A foreign policy announced in the Midlothian campaign was likely to be concerned with 'love of freedom' and 'a desire to give it scope'.[3]

The rise of parliamentary government in Europe affected the conduct of international relations. In the British case, it was often invoked by statesmen to justify a line they wished to pursue; but it was also a constraining factor. The traditional policy towards Turkey was made more difficult to pursue as a result of the Bulgarian agitation. The entente policy pursued by the Liberal government after 1906 was hard to explain to parliament, not only because of the Liberals' own differences, but because publicity would intensify commitment. The failure of the policy was indeed to be blamed on secrecy by those critics who formed the Union of Democratic Control. Whether a foreign policy could be pursued in a parliamentary way was in fact doubtful.

The rise of parliamentary government also affected colonial and imperial policy. It added to the links between metropolis and dependency. It also added to their complexity, and indeed it produced contradictions. It could at times wind the affairs of the colony closely into the politics of the mother country. That has no parallel in the present day. The responsibility that may be felt in one country for the affairs of another has now no such dimension. Perhaps that makes the past the more worthy of study rather than the reverse.

The position differed from country to country, though the nineteenth century everywhere saw an advance in parliamentary influence. The affairs of India were debated in the British House of Commons, though 'double government' was not displaced until, after the mutiny, the East India Company was finally abolished in 1858. The affairs of the Netherlands India, however, were not so debated before 1848. They were a matter for the king and his advisers, and not for the States-General. Even after 1848, there were arguments for caution. 'Some people desire', declared J. M. de Kempenaer, 'that much should be left to be controlled by legislation in the mother country, but we warn: don't risk it, because you do not know that land, nor its people, nor its needs, nor the various circumstances which have to be taken into account when making such laws.'[4] The Philippines case was different again. Briefly its Spanish subjects had been represented in the Cortes, but that had ceased in 1837.

The directions taken by parliamentary debate might well be varied, but it was at least likely to open up a range of opinions on colonial affairs, and in general to enhance a sense of responsibility. The States-General, once permitted to discuss the Indies, would no doubt listen to hypocrites like Droogstoppel in Multatuli's novel, *Max Havelaar*. Other voices, however, would also be raised; that of Van Hoevell, for example. Sir James Brooke would be defended in the House of Commons, but he would also be attacked. Governments could lie or evade. The British government laid papers, but it might edit or abbreviate them, as Palmerston did. But it recognised that it had to offer a rationale for what it was doing. The exercise of power was challenged, if not bridled.

Defending the East India Company in 1852, J. S. Mill thought that 'the public opinion of one country is scarcely any security for the good government of another'.[5] But a parliamentary system might make for less arbitrary rule: the actions of governments might become more open, and more accountable, though possibly more devious. But the actual abandonment of the colonial relationship was quite a different matter. There the system might work in a different direction.

A king is in a better position to bargain possessions away than a state, let alone a nation. The play of parliamentary and public interest may indeed work against so decisive an act. That would be the case particularly if the government of the day had an insecure basis in the parliamentary assembly.

The Americans acquired the Philippines in doubt and continued retention was justified by insistence that the ultimate aim was independence. Realising that turned out to be a long process. Indeed it was only when the depression spurred on the desire to destroy competition from Philippines sugar that Congress moved towards what became the Commonwealth Act. That provided a timetable for independence.

The British moved to grant dependencies self-government and dominion status within the Commonwealth. In one case, Burma, they accepted the goal of absolute independence: this the AFPFL leadership had set. Parliament was the scene of a bitter protest from the Opposition leader, Winston Churchill, whose father, Lord Randolph Churchill, had been Secretary of State when Upper Burma was acquired in 1885–6. 'I certainly did not expect to see U Aung San, whose hands were dyed with British blood and loyal Burmese blood, marching up the steps of Buckingham Palace as the plenipotentiary of the Burmese Government.'[6] But Labour had a large majority, and in any case in general British decolonisation was a bipartisan policy. That it could be presented for the most part as an adjustment – from empire to Commonwealth – helped. It was also true that the British had so large an empire that withdrawal from no one part of it seemed to be fatal.

The Dutch were in a different position. For them, the Indies was traditionally a source of wealth and prestige; and postwar they were thus extraordinarily tenacious. But it is clear that the parliamentary system made any adjustment more difficult. The Hoge Veluwe talks were abortive in part because an election was due. No government could campaign in the face of an accusation that it had given the colonies away. After the second Police Action, Dirk Stikker, the Foreign Minister, 'emphasized political difficulty for coalition Netherlands Government [to] accept detailed resolution adopted by S[ecurity] C[ouncil]'.[7] The retention of West New Guinea in the final 1949 deal was designed to win over opposition to the recognition of independence. Conservatives could be told that the Dutch flag still flew in Southeast Asia. Governments that had to hold majorities together – unlike the British Labour Government – were driven to pursue conservative policies, and big steps, when finally made, had also to involve compromises, damaging though they might be to long-term relationships.

Something similar might also be said of French Indo-China. True, it was no sheet-anchor for France; but, as in its acquisition, so in its retention, 'grandeur' played a part. 'It is better to pronounce the word Independence at the opportune moment than to be thrown out', Henri Laurentie of the French Colonial Office suggested,[8] but it was difficult to do that at a time when France was attempting to recover from defeat and humiliation. It was difficult, too, for governments of the day, anxious to retain support in the chamber, to offer broadly based, conciliatory and forward-looking colonial policies, lest they be accused of abandoning French interests: 'internal politics in France have been even more responsible for the failure to reach a solution than the intricacies of the situation on the spot'.[9]

The prospect of independence might emphasise a parliament's disposition to retain rather than to relinquish or even to reform. Once independence was gained, however, the metropolitan government lost its formal responsibility for the erstwhile dependency. Indeed independence, so long sought, would not brook interference. Concern about the behaviour of governments in ex-colonial states nevertheless made itself felt. It worked through the media, now much extended in scope and audience, and through Amnesty and NGOs. The formal government ties had gone and with them the possibility of using parliamentary responsibility. Attempts were made to tie human rights to aid and even trade. That was an inadequate substitute for the imperial connexions of the past. Inadequate as they were, those had made some assertion of responsibility possible. But their day had gone.

In their time the imperial governments had given their colonies only a limited experience of parliamentary rule and, indeed, of other freedoms, like that of the press, that helped to check abuses at home. The parliaments set up in the former colonies were weakened by that lack of experience. The chance that they would be in a position to check abuses of their fellow citizens by their fellow citizens was in turn limited.

Some form of parliament was everywhere retained, associated as it was with the gaining of independence and with modernity. But the reality of parliamentary practice was less apparent. In some cases, indeed, the colonial governments had left behind machinery that the independent governments continued to use. Even where that was not the case, the new governments might resemble the old in approach. Suharto's Indonesia echoed some of the Dutch practices of the 1920s and 1930s.

The attempts of outsiders to intervene might not only be inadequate: they might be counterproductive. The Karens had felt deprived of the last hope of outside help when Burma failed to join the Commonwealth, and Britain found it impossible to tie financial support for a beleaguered Rangoon government to better treatment for the rebels. As Nehru put it at Colombo early in 1950: 'the position was extremely delicate, as the Burmese Government naturally resented any attempt to interfere in their domestic affairs'.[10] Such attempts could be depicted as a renewal of imperialism. Attempted interventions of this nature were also to prompt some Asian leaders to redefine human rights or to develop 'Asian' versions of them. ●

---

1   C. Thorne, *The Issue of War*, London: Hamilton, 1985, p. xi.
2   Cf Alfred P. Rubin, *Piracy, Paramountcy and Protectorates*, Kuala Lumpur: Penerbit Universiti Malaya, 1974, pp. 6 ff.
3   quoted G. A. Craig and Alexander L. George, *Force and Statecraft*, New York: Oxford University Press, 1983, p. 265.
4   quoted C. Fasseur, *The Politics of Colonial Exploitation*, Ithaca, NY: Southeast Asia Program, Cornell University, 1992, p. 103.
5   quoted P. J. Durrans, 'The House of Commons and India 1847–1880', *Journal of the Royal Asiatic Society*, 1 (1982), p. 32.
6   Hansard, House of Commons, Vol. 443, cols. 1836ff, 5 November 1947.
7   Kirk/SofS, 9/2/49, 213. *Foreign Relations of the United States*, 1949, VII, p. 218.
8   quoted S. Tonnesson, *The Vietnamese Revolution of 1945*, London: Sage, 1991, p. 367.
9   Dening/Templer, 18/12/48. FO371/75960 [F1539/1015/86].
10 FMM (50) 7th, 12/1/50. CAB 133/78, Public Record Office, London.

NATIONALISM

Benedict Anderson wrote of nationalism as 'an imagined political community'.[1] William J. Duiker has offered the suggestion that nationalism should be seen as a process. 'Nationalism ... is not a phenomenon that appears suddenly. It is the result of a process by which a people become conscious of themselves as a separate national entity in the modern world, a process by which they become willing to transfer their primary loyalty from the village, or the region, or the monarch, to the nation-state...'[2] Stage by stage, a people becomes conscious of a sense of community as a nation, and of its position as a nation among nations, in what becomes a world of nation-states.

Duiker's suggestion is useful in a number of ways. It encompasses the shift in loyalties that is likely to occur. It distinguishes the articulation of those loyalties among the elite and among the masses. It suggests that nationalism distinguishes one community from another. It argues that the general aspiration of nationalists is to independence in a world of nation-states. The concept is made still more useful if it is recognised that it offers a model but not necessarily a time-frame: the processes may be compressed and the sequences disturbed. There may also be a geographical variant.

Nationalism arises in Western Europe, in particular in France, also in Britain, though the issue is complicated by the existence of a United Kingdom, in some way multinational. It emerges, in a sense, because a state exists, rather than because a state should exist. It emerges as a result of a sense of community developed over centuries, though it may also be prompted by a catastrophe, like the revolution of 1789 or the war against Napoleon. A state of this kind would initially not have been built upon a national principle but a monarchical one. The shift to a national principle might or might not involve the elimination of the monarchy, but it was certainly likely to change its position. Subjects were likely to become nationals, if not citizens.

In this time-frame the Duiker model is in some sense stood on its head. But the nationalism of these countries was an example to others, in which the model might apply more exactly. Indeed the actuality of these states might provoke a sense of nationalism among others. The German romantic nationalism of the early nineteenth century was a reaction to the French version, associated with invasion and revolution, and its state was more corporatist. That version was known to nationalists in Southeast Asia, and to some of them, in Indonesia for example, it seemed more relevant than the French.

In the German case, moreover, it might be thought that the working of the Duiker model was upset by time as well as geography. The unification of at least part of German-speaking Europe was achieved before the process was mature. Bismarck used nationalism to create the Second Reich; but the sense of community remained deficient. His successors used nationalist policies to try to develop a sense of community in the face of social division. Their right-wing pan-German critics wanted to go further and create a nation-state that included the German-speakers so far excluded. Again the example might seem relevant to a post-colonial world.

Italy is divergent, too, perhaps still more so. Nationalists had laboured to secure unification in some form or other, papally-led, republican, monarchical. They failed. What brought unification was foreign intervention, and indeed a shift of power among other European states. Wars with France, and then with Prussia, led to the withdrawal of Austria from almost all the Italian-speaking lands. It was that, as well as Piedmontese leadership, that led to unification. Somehow the new state so created seemed not to fulfil the hopes of the Risorgimento. No doubt those hopes had been inflamed by undue optimism. But it was also true that, in a sense, unification had come too soon. The Italian state had to make the Italian nation. And some found it difficult to wait while it did. This example, too, has some Southeast Asian parallels.

In other parts of Europe, the Duiker model might apply. Yet almost everywhere nationalism was in part generated by antagonism. There were rulers who were, or who now seemed, alien; empires that had to be broken up; oppressors who had to be overthrown. That might distort the process. The elite might be tempted to compromise, or it might attempt premature revolution. It might fail, or it might win premature success as a result of other factors. Nationalisms, after all, existed in a world of states, not yet a world of nation-states. The leaders of such states might intervene, for or against.

Finally, of course, nationalism was a disintegrative as well as an integrative force. It was not merely that nationalism might undermine or overthrow an alien or imperial regime. Nationalisms themselves might contend. Even in the established states of the West, there were nationalisms that countervailed that of the majority. The French revolutionaries faced that in Brittany. Whether or not the United Kingdom reconciled the Welsh and the Scots, it failed to reconcile the Irish. The aspirant nationalisms themselves contained within them rival aspirant nationalisms. Not every nation could indeed have a state. Rather every state sought to be a nation-state.

In Southeast Asia nationalism was both reactive and creative, constructive and destructive. Generally nationalists were reacting against colonial rulers, seeking to destroy the colonial regimes. At the same time, they were domesticating the nationalist idea, and in some sense, even when they were struggling with their rulers, collaborating in a common endeavour.

Colonial rulers provoked nationalism by providing education but not opportunity. Education they had to provide, if only in the interests of modernisation; but they were less ready to share power with the educated. Limiting the provision of tertiary education led the same way. The elite from Sumatra and Java met each other in Batavia or in Bandung or in the Netherlands itself. 'Those who studied abroad figured particularly strongly in the leadership of the early Indonesian nationalist movement.'[3] In the metropolis, indeed, nationalists felt freer than at home. 'It is as if another sky is arching out over their heads. They became aware here of the feeling of freedom ... The truth is that we have been set free from the colonial hypnosis,' Hatta wrote. '... From here we can see the *colonial* truth clearly.'[4]

Duiker's remarks were offered in the introduction to his book on nationalism in Vietnam in the twentieth century. Among the Southeast Asian countries the Vietnamese were perhaps the people who might most readily be said, though still with some risk of anachronism, to have had over a long period of history a sense of identity, if not indeed of nationality. That had been derived, in a somewhat paradoxical way, from their initial incorporation in the Chinese empire. Their breakaway was sustained by their earlier cohesion. Their cohesion was also stimulated by their determination to maintain the independence won from their Chinese overlord. In subsequent centuries, it encouraged the Vietnamese to expand southwards at the expense of other peoples, the Chams, the Khmers. Maintaining the unity of the elongated state that developed tested the political ingenuity of Vietnamese rulers, but a common sense of being Vietnamese endured. On the arrival of the French imperialists the Nguyen dynasty failed to turn it to account, but the French could not eliminate it. There were divisions among the Vietnamese, but the impact of the foreigners, French, Japanese and Americans, in the end tended to reduce them rather than the reverse. The sense of being Vietnamese became the basis of a nationalist struggle for independence and unification.

The chief mainland states of Southeast Asia indeed have a continuity in their history that conduces to a sense of nationality, in turn the ready basis of a nationalist movement. The Burman peoples had a common language, common traditions, common customs, and a sense of identity that survived political upsets and changes of dynasty. The stage-by-stage British Indian conquest did not destroy that unity. On the contrary it tended to provoke a nationalist opposition, which also turned to account examples, formulae, and modes of organisation derived from British India. Burma differed from Vietnam, however, inasmuch as, to a far greater extent, the frontiers of the state contained minority peoples, who also retained a sense of identity and in some cases, like that of the Karens, developed their own nationalism, partly as a result of Western education.

The third of the major mainland states, Siam/Thailand, also had a long and continuous history. Its people, too, had a sense of identity that might approximate to a sense of nationality. In other ways, Siam differed from Burma and Vietnam. Particularly after it surrendered to the Europeans parts of the territory it claimed in Laos, Cambodia, and the Malay Peninsula, it did not have a minority problem on the scale of Burma's. Moreover, partly as a result of those territorial concessions, but also as a result of a wise statesmanship, it maintained its independence of European control. That meant that the development of nationalism was less precipitate; it also had a different focus. Sometimes, indeed, it was xenophobic, in regard to the Chinese, for example. It also focused on the monarchy, which had played so large a role in preserving the independence in which the Thais rightly took so much pride.

In the rest of Southeast Asia, the states have no such political continuity. Their frontiers are even more completely those created by the colonial powers. Within those frontiers, more of the sense of nationalism was bred by opposition to those colonial powers. Even when independence was secured, it was perhaps to a greater extent a result of changes in the international distribution of power. Independence was not only won; it came partly as a gift from others. Like the Italians, the Indonesians had still to work on making a nation, even after a state has been created.

In the Philippines, the elite had developed a sense of being 'Filipino', a word it had appropriated over a much longer period. Yet the independent Philippine state was hardly a nation-state. First, the elite itself was divided regionally. Second, the loyalty of the masses was to family and to patron, rather than to region, let alone to nation. Some 40.6 per cent of heads of farm families had no formal education, a 1951–2 survey suggested.[5] Education was in any case delivered in English and later Tagalog: in non-Tagalog provinces there were few reading materials, and the effectiveness of broadcasting was limited. Third, the Muslims had no clear allegiance to the Philippines, and indeed began to talk of and to organise and fight for their own national liberation, helped by Islamic states and subsidies.

Malaysia and Singapore had an even shorter history as states. Only after 1946 did the British create a single government over what Swettenham had imaginatively called British Malaya. The addition of Sarawak and Sabah came only with the creation of Malaysia in 1963. The understandings that were involved further limited the development of a sense of nationality. Malaya advanced to independence through a deal between Malay and Chinese leaders. Federal Malaysia gave Sarawak and Sabah areas of autonomy.

Singapore it was never thought could be independent, let alone national. It had been separated from Malaya after the war in order to make it easier to secure an understanding between Malays and Chinese and in order to retain a base for British activity in Southeast Asia. That separation was seen as temporary, for neither the British nor educated Singaporeans thought that the island state could survive on its own. That conviction helped to take it into Malaysia. But, that experiment failing, it turned out that, given the new circumstances of the 1960s and 1970s and dynamic leadership, it could survive. It could even aspire to be national: it celebrated a national day; its university became the National University of Singapore.

Our world is a world of states, even, as it is called, a world of nations. But, equal in status, they are utterly disparate in size, wealth, and power. The exertion of influence by one over the other is thus unavoidable, even proper and in a sense desirable. The system would not work even as well as it does without a recognition that the equality and inequality are combined and independence by the small can only be sustained by recognising that it is incomplete. But there is, of course, a risk that the powerful are dissatisfied with this abnegation. What checks are there on them?

In some ways barriers in the way of the powerful are now being thrown down. The pressure to establish free trade echoes, for example, the aspiration of the British in the days of their economic predominance. In some sense that may of course, as then, limit the aspiration of major powers to exert political control. But there is the risk that it provokes a reaction, and not merely a protectionist one. Is the assertion of nationality not in part a reaction to the pressures for globalisation, reflecting a concern that social identity will be lost? 'The threat to independence in the late twentieth century from the new electronics could be greater than was colonialism itself... The new media have the power to penetrate more deeply into a "receiving" culture than any previous manifestation of Western technology.'[6] The reaction might produce another tyranny. The assertion of nationalism could swamp the liberties of individuals, the identities of lesser communities.

In other ways again we have disarmed major powers, and again that is not all advantage. Intervention in the imperialist world might have resulted from greed and acquisitiveness. It also resulted from a wish to bring order. And that might not simply be an imperial order. It might be designed to remedy genuine abuses, most famously, for example, to put down slavery. Moreover, if some interventions led to formal acquisition, there was in the imperial system some formal provision of accountability. Governors could be called to account; parliaments would receive reports. Intervention is now discredited, and acquisition ruled out. But that leaves a gap, filled imperfectly by the efforts of the UN and by NGOs. And our emphasis on world-wide economic activity has made it difficult to impose barriers against items that are virtually slave-produced.

It may be that nevertheless the world has gained. What went along with imperialism, and more particularly with empire, was an attitude of mind that was often, though not always, what we would now call racist. But that has proved more difficult to overthrow than empire itself. It may indeed be that such attitudes are not diminished, but even encouraged by the end of imperialism. Are the relations among human societies to be determined by attitudes that seem to make for violence that is more difficult to bridle? ●

1   B. Anderson, *Imagined Communities*, London and New York: Verso, 1991, p. 6.

2   W. J. Duiker, *The Rise of Nationalism in Vietnam, 1900–1941*, Ithaca: Cornell University Press, 1976, p. 15.

3   J. A. Scholte, 'The International Construction of Indonesian Nationhood, 1930–1950', in Hans Antlov and S. Tonnesson, eds, *Imperial Policy and Southeast Asian Nationalism*, London: Curzon, 1995, p. 206.

4   M. Rose, *Indonesia Free*, Ithaca: Cornell University, Southeast Asia Program, p. 18.

5   F. L. Starner, *Magsaysay and the Philippine Peasantry*, Berkeley: University of California Press, 1961.
6   Aubrey Smith, *The Geopolitics of Information*, quoted Said, pp. 91–2.

THE JAPANESE

The impact of the Japanese invasion in Southeast Asia depended both on the actions of the Japanese and on the context within which they acted in the various territories they penetrated.

Their interest in Southeast Asia was of long standing: it had both an ideological and a practical background. The ideology was tied to the pan-Asianism that was associated with the Meiji restoration, though it did not dominate it. That event was, of course, connected with the dramatic changes in East Asia in the 1840s. The Tokugawa policy of seclusion had been adopted for domestic reasons and had indeed become a national policy. But it did not depend only on acceptance at home: it also depended on international acceptance. That was for a long time forthcoming. In some sense it was indeed a Dutch policy. The leading European maritime nation at the time the policy was adopted, the Dutch were granted a unique privilege under it – access to Nagasaki – and they were the more ready to accept it inasmuch as their rivals were thus excluded. 'The Dutch did their best to cut foreigners off from Japan, and this helped create the illusion of a closed country from the 1640s onward.'[1] The Russians threatened the policy in the late eighteenth and early nineteenth centuries, but did not carry their threat through, though it alarmed the Japanese. The defeat of China by the British in the war of 1840–2 signalled a real shift in East Asia, and suggested that the seclusion policy could no longer be sustained. The arrival of Perry and his Black Ships in the following decade drove the message home. Treaties were made. Those of 1858 that opened Japan's ports to foreign trade were the signal for a ten-year struggle among the Japanese that fully overthrew the Tokugawa and produced the restoration.

Associated with these changes were changes in the Japanese attitude to the outside world. Before the Meiji restoration, those that called for change within Japan also expected change in Japan's position in the world. In some current frustration nurtured large future ambitions. 'With proper spirit and discipline on our part', Sato Nobuhiro argued, 'China would crumble and fall like a house of sand within five to seven years.'[2] In the event more moderate policies were followed, seeking to undo the unequal treaties, but otherwise involving in general a restrained approach, and one unlikely to offend the British. Even the oligarchs of the 1870s, however, had their ambitions, while their critics thought they were far from ambitious enough.

There were also differences of approach. The crucial fact was the weakness of China. A pan-Asian approach envisaged working with a revived China so as to avoid the dominance in East Asia of powers from outside the region. The more realistic policy was a more direct one. Japan must itself take steps to avoid the dominance of the West, if need be at China's expense. In a sense, it must join the imperialists, though in order to limit them.

Both these objectives affected Southeast Asia. Japan's imperialism initially had Korea as its target. But, while in 1876 it secured a treaty there like the one the French secured in Vietnam, it initially focused on Taiwan. The policy was controversial at home. 'The basis of our government is not yet firmly established ... We must build our industry, our exports, etc. It is our most urgent business.'[3] The dominant oligarchs in fact preferred a more cautious policy, pending Japan's self-strengthening and modernisation. This policy was abandoned in the 1890s. The oligarchs now met an elected Diet, in which the pressure for expansion was strong, and they felt able to respond to it. The advance of Russia, and the weakness of China, provided a further external motivation. Korea must be secured before the Russians interposed. Following its triumph in the Sino-Japanese war of 1894–5, Japan obtained China's recognition that Korea was independent. It acquired Taiwan. That brought it to the confines of Southeast Asia. Some radicals wanted to intervene in the Philippines rebellion against Spain. In the event the US intervened and stayed. That put a barrier in the way of further imperial expansion southward on the part of Japan.

Japan's activities had, however, another effect in Southeast Asia. In 1895 the Triple Intervention forced it to return Port Arthur to China, but China's weakness led to the Battle for the Concessions, and then to the Boxer Uprising. In turn that prompted the introduction of foreign troops into China. The Russians seemed unwilling to leave Manchuria. Indications that they might also have designs on Korea led the Japanese again to act. In their war with Russia, they enjoyed success beyond their own and others' expectations. The Russian fleet was destroyed at Tsushima. Bitter battles on land testified to Japanese audacity and determination. Russia's defeat was seen as a victory by an Asian power over a European one. In Southeast Asia that stirred nascent nationalist feeling: it seemed to show what could be done. Was there 'some kind of abacus', the hero in Pramoedya's novel asks, to 'use to calculate how many dozens of years it will take the Javanese to reach the same level as the Japanese'?[4]

The impact of the Japanese on Southeast Asia in the Second World War was felt mainly, of course, through their invasion of the region, but it reflected the idealist side of their approach as well as the realist. Their arms now overthrow the long-established colonial system in the region. But their venture still retained elements of the pan-Asian approach, and that affected the reception their armies and their administrators were afforded in the various territories.

Their approach had indeed become yet more realist over the inter-war decades. For much of the 1920s it had been more pacific. That was not so much the result of a pan-Asian idealism as of an adaptation to an altered Western approach. 'The Western Powers had taught the Japanese the game of poker', as Matsuoka put it, 'but . . . after acquiring most of the chips they pronounced the game immoral and took up contract bridge'.[5] The democracies had won the First World War: that seemed, to those who wanted a stronger Japan, an endorsement of democracy. The approach to international relations had, despite the failures of Wilson, become more Wilsonian. '. . . party leaders endorsed "international cooperation" in the 1920s because their supreme commitment was to the defense and enhancement of Japan's imperial interests.'[6] As a result of these trends, the Japanese governments pursued policies of commercial rather than imperial expansion. Shidehara's policy of 'China friendship' was preferred. China was on the way to modernisation, and Japan should welcome that, rather than obstruct it. KMT (Kuomintang) policies were following a 'trail once blazed by Japan in her struggle to emerge from a position of international inequality'.[7]

Neither the approach of the Western powers, nor that of the Japanese, appeased the impatience of the Chinese nationalists. That was initially fuelled by the alliance of the Kuomintang with the fledgling Chinese Communist Party. When that broke up, it was fuelled by the KMT's anxiety to avoid the criticism that it was unwilling to resist the imperialists. The impact of the urge to undo the unequal treaties, and to regain full sovereignty, was felt initially by the British, so much of whose enterprise was based in the Yangtse region. But as the Northern March reached the north, the interests of the Japanese came into question. To extreme Japanese nationalists Shidehara's approach seemed inadequate: in 1928 officers in the Kwantung army took action on their own initiative, eliminating the Manchurian warlord. That only prompted his son to proclaim adherence to the KMT and thus intensify the clash between Chinese nationalism and Japanese imperialism. The depression after 1929, which hit the Japanese economy hard, made friendship with China yet more difficult to pursue. The 1931 'incident' followed. Internally Japan shifted to a more bureaucratic approach to decision-making in the hope, it may be, that it would lead to greater moderation in foreign policy. In fact foreign policy tended to become the sum total of what the most important ministers wanted.

The Japanese engaged in an ambitious venture in China. They moved into it without a careful calculation: they failed to attain their objectives, but expanded them. The undeclared war of 1937 illustrated the paradox. Faced with a vast task, the Japanese needed vast resources. The military thought in terms of a long build-up, avoiding incidents meanwhile. The Konoe government adopted a bolder approach. An attempt was to be made to secure resources in China which alone would make the pursuit of Japan's objectives possible in the longer term. The all-out endeavour did not succeed. 'Konoe's summer gamble – ending the incident with one immediate blow and paying for the effort later – had failed.'[8] What it did was once more to expand Japan's objectives without attaining them. It also alarmed other powers, though not to the extent that they effectively intervened. Indeed they tended to conclude, as did Sir John Brenan at the British Foreign Office in 1938, that 'in the long run the Chinese would be more than a match for the Japanese and the extent of Japan's military dominion on the mainland will be the measure of her difficulties in the years to come'.[9]

These endeavours, though in one sense a new extreme in Japanese imperialism, were still shrouded in a form of idealism. Japan was liberating Asia from the West. In 1934 Amau spoke of a Monroe doctrine for East Asia. By 1936 the rhetoric had taken on the colouring of Japanese militarism. Konoe in turn spoke at the end of 1938 of a 'New Order' in East Asia, a notion again with a Western parallel, borrowing the rhetoric of the European dictators. Pan-Asianism had not, however, been abandoned. The approach to puppet rulers – first in Manchukuo, then in China itself – was supported by it. The new focus on Southeast Asia was presented in the form of a Greater East Asia Co-Prosperity Sphere.

Southeast Asia had been in Japanese minds before this, of course, both in terms of pan-Asian idealism, and in the terms of imperialism. The mutiny of Indian troops in Singapore in 1915 had led the Japanese to proffer assistance to the British. 'The pitiful state of a colony without effective power was brought home to me', wrote a Japanese journalist. 'What', Tsukuda asked his Tokyo readers in 1916, 'is the significance to be attached to the fact that the flag of the Rising Sun was set up in the centre of Singapore?'[10] Postwar the Japanese had returned to Netherlands India, the Dutch less apprehensive of them than they had been during the war. Their interest in oil particularly focused their attention on Borneo and Sumatra, and the Manchuria incident of 1931 revived Dutch apprehensions about them. Might the Japanese not make a sudden descent on those parts of the Indies? Once they were there, it might not be possible to get them out.

It was only in the middle of the decade, however, that Southeast Asia began to feature in the programmes of the Japanese, in particular as a result of the interest of the imperial Japanese navy. That was at once nervous about access to its resources, and apprehensive about trying to guarantee it. Japan's oil mostly came from the Americas and had to cross the American-dominated Pacific. A more secure source, nearer at hand, would make Japan better able to pursue its policies in Asia without the risk of American interposition. Securing such a source, however, might not be feasible if the Americans stepped in, and taking on the Americans was not something the navy could readily contemplate. The Fundamental Principles of 1936 thus endorsed 'footsteps' in the south.[11]

What turned those footsteps into the heavy print of invaders' boots was, above all, war in Europe. The frustrations the Japanese faced in China indeed made them look towards Southeast Asia. Continued resistance in China they tended to blame on support for the KMT from the West, and that prompted them to attempt to restrict supplies from Burma and from Indo-China. The opening of the war in Europe, and in particular the dramatic collapse of France in June 1940, led them to step up their pressure. The Burma Road was closed, and they moved into northern Vietnam, though without displacing the Vichy regime.

The fortunes of the war in Europe also led the Japanese to focus on the south. It was not merely that the European regimes might be open to pressure. Still more important was the build-up in American power that followed the collapse of France, coupled with the growing indications that the US attached more importance to the fate of Southeast Asia than it had to the fate of China. The Americans wanted to keep British resistance to the Germans alive as long as possible. Keeping open to them the resources of Asia and Australasia became an important consideration in US policy. 'The fate of Britain in Europe was inextricably linked with the fate of Britain in the Orient. And our policy of aiding Britain to resist Germany was not confined to Europe. Any weakening of Britain, as by a Japanese attack in the Orient which interfered with the supplies she needed from the Indian Ocean and Australasia area for her struggle in Europe, would be indirectly an attack on us, and could not leave us indifferent.'[12] The Americans were thus more likely to resist Japanese dominance of Southeast Asia. At the same time, the Americans had recognised that they had also to build up their own defences, and they resolved to build a two-ocean navy. That would enable them more effectively to interpose in the path of Japanese expansion.

In a sense the Japanese were faced in 1941 with the kind of choice they had presented themselves with in 1937. In order to carry on the struggle with any chance of success, they felt obliged to take a gamble. That might secure the resources needed; it might merely expand the war. But the gamble of 1941, by contrast to that of 1937, involved an attack on the major maritime powers, to their surprise, indeed, on both of them at once. 'The firmer your attitude and ours', Churchill had mistakenly told Roosevelt, 'the less chance of their taking the plunge'.[13]

'Determined to find a way of life in a fateful situation and to see justice and right, we have challenged the oppression of Britain and the United

States', the leading article in the February 1942 issue of the popular magazine *Kaizo* proclaimed. 'We must ponder carefully how in India, Burma, the Straits Settlements, Borneo and Malaya, we are to reconstruct in the wake of people who have merely been extortionists. Our policies for the people we shall free, will require sagacity and great boldness.'[14]

The Japanese invasions of Southeast Asia overthrew the colonial system. That in itself had more impact, no doubt, than the residual pan-Asianism it carried with it. Pan-Asianism, however, expanded the welcome the Japanese initially received in Indonesia, and it consolidated their connexion with the Burman radicals, though it meant far less to the Filipino elite, already promised independence in 1946. The legacy of their war in China brought the Japanese no welcome from the Chinese communities. Indeed they were rightly apprehensive of the policies the Japanese would pursue towards them.

In the course of the war, the other communities were reminded of the limits of pan-Asianism by the harshness of the conditions under which the new empire laboured or which it imposed. But it did set up regimes that would counter the return of the colonial powers, and that would in some sense tie Southeast Asia and Japan together in the future. 'If the Japanese can make their forced withdrawal seem to be a further invasion of Asia by imperial white powers, they can leave behind them the foundation for another effort sometime in the future', George Kerr commented.[15] The Gaimusho argued that 'the ideological foundation developed during the war of liberation in Greater East Asia by the Empire, is, regardless of the course of the war, an eventuality which even the enemy must follow and accept.'[16]

Undoubtedly the setting-up of pseudo-independent regimes – in Burma, as in the Philippines, in 1943 – and the Koiso proposals for an independent Indonesia in 1944 were designed not only to enlist support in the war but to make the return of the colonial powers more impracticable. In that they succeeded. In the future Japan was able to deal with a post-colonial Southeast Asia and thus to approach it on state-to-state and regional bases. The policies and practices it had adopted during its occupation had not, however, been so sagacious as *Kaizo* had hoped. The post-colonial entente with Japan was not built on ties of gratitude or sympathy, though it reflected a Shidehara approach to foreign policy. ●

---

1   Bob Tadashi Wakabayashi, *Anti-Foreignism and Western Learning in Early-Modern Japan*, Cambridge Mass.: Harvard University Press, 1986, pp. 64–5.

2   quoted W. G. Beasley, *The Meiji Restoration*, Stanford: Stanford University Press, 1972, p. 80.

3   Okubo Toshimichi, quoted J. Pittau, *Political Thought in Early Meiji Japan*, Cambridge Mass.: Harvard University Press, 1967, pp. 29–30.

4   *This Earth of Mankind*, trans Max Lane, Melbourne: Penguin, 1982/1991, p. 315.

5   Matsuoka, quoted Richard D. Burns and E. M. Bennett, eds, *Diplomats in Crisis*, Santa Barbara, ABC-Clio, 1974, p. 276.

6   Gordon M. Berger, *Parties Out of Power in Japan 1931–1941*, Princeton: Princeton University Press, 1977, p. 354.

7   James B. Crowley, in J. W. Morley, ed., *Japan's Foreign Policy*, New York and London: Columbia University Press, 1974, p. 102.

8   Michael A. Barnhart, *Japan Prepares for Total War*, Ithaca: Cornell University Press, 1987, p. 103.

9   quoted W. Roger Louis, *British Strategy in the Far East*, Oxford: Clarendon, 1971, p. 249.

10   Notes from M. Tsukuda, *From Nanyo*, in WO/FO, 21/1/18. FO371/3235[13287].

11   James B. Crowley, *Japan's Quest for Autonomy*, Princeton University Press, 1966, p. 296.

12   Cordell Hull, *Memoirs*, London: Hodder, 1948, II, p.1059.

13   quoted N. Graebner, 'Hoover, Roosevelt and the Japanese', in D. Borg and S. Okamoto, eds, *Pearl Harbor as History*, New York and London: Columbia University Press, 1973, p. 51.

14   quoted Usui Katsumi in Ian Nish, ed., *Anglo-Japanese Alienation, 1919–1952*, Cambridge: Cambridge University Press, 1982, p. 96.

15   quoted Akira Iriye, *Power and Culture*, Cambridge Mass.: Harvard University Press, 1981, p. 166.

16   quoted H. Benda et al., *Japanese Military Administration in Indonesia*, New Haven: Southeast Asia Studies, Yale University, 1985, p. 242.

GAINING INDEPENDENCE

Independence is one of those words, like nationalism, which are often used in political discourse and the meaning of which seems clear. Closer examination suggests that frequent usage does not imply clarity. Moreover, the meaning of the word will vary, in particular cases in substance and in general over time. Realising that will, however, make it easier to give an intelligible explanation of the gaining of independence. It will help to explain why independence is more easily won on some occasions than others and by some states than others.

It is not inappropriate to approach the task of definition indirectly. 'Independence' means after all non-dependence: it describes a position of not being rather than of being. An independent state might thus be one that is not dependent on another state. That would also mean that its governance is not dependent on another state, and that its governors are not provided by others. In some way or ways it produces its own.

Dependence perhaps implies a question of degree. Independence seems absolute. A state might thus be more or less dependent, dependent in some ways and not in others. An independent state, by contrast, would have no such ties at all. But it may be more intelligible, if not more logical, to regard independence, too, as a matter of degree, so that a state may be more or less independent. The apparent illogicality is reduced by introducing the issue of perception.

The perception of independence may be considered from two points of view. From the point of view of the governed, the government of the day might still appear remote, if not alien, even if it were of indigenous origin: its dependence or independence hard to assess, perhaps even irrelevant. In this discussion the second point of view, that of other states, is a more significant consideration. A state will be seen as independent by other states. None of them may be absolutely independent. What indicates independence is acceptance by other states, in Western diplomacy a matter of recognition; in the post-war world, more often than not, accompanied by another process, acceptance as a member of the United Nations. Independence becomes a matter of convention.

Over time the concept has indeed changed. It belongs to the system of states that emerged in Europe with the collapse of the Holy Roman Empire and the failure of would-be successor superordinates, Napoleonic Empire, the happily much-less-than-1,000-year-old Reich. European states developed a pattern of diplomacy based on independence, recognition, sovereignty. Theoretically they were equal, even though they were not equal in power. They sent ambassadors to each other's courts, not tribute missions.

The development of such a system in Europe both excluded the rest of the world and invited it in. While it appeared to be susceptible of world-wide application, it grew up in Europe. There were unspoken assumptions about acceptance and recognition. There were, or came to be, criteria, and these varied over time. A state had, perhaps, to be capable of defending itself. Were there other conditions of viability? Did a state also have to meet certain standards? Could its government be revolutionary? Must it be monarchical? Must it provide stability? Must it be democratic? If independence was a matter of convention, that convention shifted on the shifting sands of time.

The expansion of Europe's contacts with the rest of the world took place even as this system was emerging in Europe. In some ways, the system, and the conventions that developed, became more exclusive to Europe, but their world-wide potential also became apparent. Was it possible, indeed, for states that were independent of one another in Europe to hold vast tracts of the rest of the world in subordination? In theory, it was; and in fact the creation of wealth and power overseas was spurred on by assertions of independence in Europe and rivalries that ensued. But in practice the European system began to take hold outside Europe as well.

Initially, indeed, the Europeans had not always assumed the imperial mantle: they had been prepared to deal with states outside Europe. Queen Elizabeth I addressed the Sultan of Aceh as 'our loving brother'.[1] That view shifted, as the gap in power widened the gap in perception, and by the early nineteenth century the Europeans were less ready to see the states in other systems as being equal, or even capable of being equal, to those in their system. They might, however, be susceptible of becoming so. That could require time; it could require guidance; it could require a period of imperial rule. But the view came to be held, especially among the British, that the whole world should come to be patterned on Europe. It would be a world of states, not of empires, dealing with each other on the basis of a theoretical equality, abiding by accepted conventions, providing stability and opportunity for trade. In the meantime other states might lose their independence, to regain it after a period of tutelage and development. Preferably, however, they would, if need be, occupy an intermediate position. 'Imperfectly civilised States', to use the phrase Palmerston applied to Siam, China and Turkey,[2] would engage in 'unequal' treaties with the Europeans.

The clash between this system and non-European systems was not less dramatic than the clash of empires. The latter indeed might be more comprehensible than the new European approach. Certainly the systems in other parts of the world for the most part differed from the one that emerged in Europe. The most famous, that of the Chinese, saw the world in terms of superordinate state and tributary states. The system was in fact not so much a system as a collection of relationships with an emperor who was the intermediary between heaven and earth. There were in fact degrees of dependence, but there could be no independence. Even the emperor himself had to have a mandate from heaven. Dealing with other states on a basis of equality, or even on a presumed basis of equality, was impossible. No state could be the equal of a state that encompassed the world as it knew it. No dependency could enter relationships that breached its tributary status. Much more was involved in 1840–2 than Britain's defeat of China. The new system challenged the old.

The concept of a world of states, the relationships among which were based on a theoretical equality, on stability, on international trade, was undermined by the great depression of the 1930s. The long period of expansion, brought about by the industrial revolution of the nineteenth century, came to a halt. Presumptions were challenged, and other views of the state, and of the relationships among states, were thrust into prominence. Some favoured Communist internationalism, compromised as it was by the Stalinist revolution. Others looked rather to blocs as the basis for future economic development. That meant also new forms of dependence and independence. Interdependence characterised the Japanese articulation if not the actuality of a Greater East Asia Co-Prosperity Sphere. Within that sphere Burma and the Philippines were granted 'independence', and Indonesia was belatedly put on the same track.

How real that independence was the Allies doubted. Japan promised 'complete independence' in 1943, the exiled Governor of Burma, Reginald Dorman-Smith observed. 'That she will not be in a position to fulfil that undertaking does not matter to her. It is good propaganda . . .'[3] In a sense, no doubt, it was again a matter of perception. Did those who were governed see their state as independent? The concept of the puppet state, developed in Manchuria, indeed shadowed these political ventures. Too obvious a control meant that the states had no perceived independence; too little control meant that they were not dependent enough. In China the puppet state gained no credibility. In Southeast Asia it could at least be seen – in Burma, if not the Philippines – as an advance on Western colonialism. But in general the Japanese concept was unconvincing: it could not provide for dependence and independence.

The US, now the major world power in succession to Britain, had never accepted the concept of economic blocs: it inherited the concepts of world trade and free access to world markets. It was this view of the world that it wished to prevail after the defeat of Germany and Japan, and which it continues to pursue.

Postwar, Asian countries came together and endorsed statements like the 'five principles of co-existence'. They were presented as a counter to Western imperialism. But in another sense they witnessed the final acceptance of the view of the world that the Europeans had begun to propound centuries before. Commenting on but also imbibing the rhetorical spirit of the Bandung conference of 1955, R. W. Parkes, the Counsellor in the British legation in Jakarta, declared that the East was 'no longer age-old, inscrutable, unchanging', but 'young, eager, drunk with new nationalism and freedom'. Let us talk of the 'glorious future that may open up for the Orient – if not disrupted by communist subversion and aggression – when Eastern nations . . . can share with us the full enjoyment of those civil and other liberties for which we, in Western history, fought with such determination and sacrifice.'[4]

Even that world did not, however, stay still. In 1945 a few states were clearly more powerful than others, and the structure of the UN recognised that. But, if the Security Council might be constituted out of the powerful (or at least victorious), the General Assembly might more readily expand. For a while, indeed, it was a slow process, because decolonisation was at first a slow process. And one reason was the question of viability. Could small states survive? Could they fulfil their obligations to other states? Could they be seen as independent? Could they be recognised? Could they become members of the UN?

In the 1950s some of the British, unlike David Marshall, thought the answer had to be negative. For Singapore, 'full self-government and independence' seemed to Patrick Dean 'doubtful propositions . . . almost the same size as the Isle of Wight . . . It cannot exist effectively as an entity on its own'.[5] By the 1970s the situation had changed out of all recognition. That was because the conventions had changed. The multinational character of the world economy and the transformation of communications did not make the state obsolete or even obsolescent. It changed its position. If none could now be seen as really independent, real independence ceased to be a criterion for acceptance by other states.

How those who were governed saw the change is less certain. In states that were democratic, it may have produced a sense of powerlessness, and thus a cynicism that endangered the stability that was fundamental to both democracy and to economic expansion. An elected government seemed less responsible to those who had elected it than to holders of power and makers of opinion outside the country. In respect of states that were not democratic, the change tended to question whether economic expansion and democratic values were indeed after all allied, as the success first of the UK, and then of the US, had tended to suggest. The criteria of civil society were eroded by assertions that the only relationships that counted among citizens were those that could be counted. The criteria of a society among nations, never fully developed or accepted, were even more readily reduced to the narrowly economic. ●

---

1   C. H. Alexandrowicz, *An Introduction to the History of the Law of Nations in the East Indies,* Oxford: Clarendon, 1967, p. 34.
2   Palmerston to Brooke, 18/12/1849. FO69/1.
3   Telegram, 9/2/43, 78. L/PO/236, India Office Records, London.
4   Some Impressions of the Bandung Conference, in Morland/Foreign Secretary, 28/4/55, 40. FO371/116983 [D.2231/319].
5   Minute, 9/3/56. FO371/123212 [D 1052/4].

DEMOCRATIC INSTITUTIONS

'Independence seems like a marriage. Who shall wait until the salary rises, say to 500 guilders and setting up house is complete? Marry first!'[1] Readiness for self-government or independence was a notion common in prewar discussions of the evolution of empire. The humourist Will Rogers imagined a conversation between President Hoover and Patrick Hurley after his visit to the Philippines in 1931. 'I asked Pat, "Pat, are they ready for Independence?" He says, "No." I say, "How can you tell when a Nation is ready for Independence?" He says, "I don't know. I never saw a Nation that was".'[2]

The elite among those who were ruled viewed the prescriptions of their rulers with a degree of cynicism that was by no means wholly unjustified. Were the criteria merely self-serving? Were they designed merely to delay the inevitable? Preparation for self-government was indeed in a sense impossible: the only preparation was the practice of it. In that way Robert Taylor turns Rogers' Hoover on his head. 'British-Indian policy', he writes, 'assumed that it was possible to find a political elite in Burma that would be able to operate a parliamentary political system in such a way as to maintain stable government, existing economic interests and the tie with the British Empire.' But, he adds, 'British policy makers failed to note that in order to allow an indigenous political elite to govern the country, that elite would have to be able to respond to the problems of its electorate.'[3] In Burma that was impossible, at least before the introduction of the 1935 constitution.

The debate was thus a muddle of principle and politics. Within it, however, the idea was, albeit obscurely, embodied that self-government meant not only good government but participatory government. Self-government meant in fact government by themselves. In a way that was part of the argument for independence. In the metropolitan countries the advance of democracy made it hard to rationalise an old-fashioned colonialism based simply on dominance, profit and extraction. 'It is the tradition of our race to be independent ourselves and to insist on political liberty, and to give it to others', Thomas Reed, MP for Swindon, was to declare in a British debate on Burma in 1947.[4] A different rationale had to be offered. In a democratic polity it was hard to deny that other peoples should not also advance politically, and that must involve the same kind of participation as the metropolitan population enjoyed. The concept of an advance to self-government became the paradoxical rationale for continued, though temporary, rule. It implied political advance in terms of political participation. It involved electoral politics. It set a time limit, though that might be imprecise.

The concept of participation, of course, extended the paradox of preparation. If self-government or independence were to depend on wider participation, then readiness for them might be a still more remote prospect. Was power to be transferred only to an elite? Or were the masses to be educated so that they might take a real part in a really democratic system? A colonial autocracy might seek to justify itself by the need for a post-colonial democracy. The chance that the former could produce the latter was, of course, slim. But if the criteria were not met in the period before self-government or independence were granted, the chances of enforcing them thereafter were likely to be still less. An outside power would be seen as interferingly neo-imperial. Only a population conscious of its rights could check an elite disposed to ignore them. An outside power might, moreover, prefer to support the elite.

The idea of participation, embedded albeit paradoxically in the concept of preparation for self-government, offered some opportunity for the population at large and some check on the elite. Participation and independence became associated. If the first had been an argument for the second in metropolitan countries, the second was an argument for the first in dependencies. A more participatory form of government showed that a country was ready for independence, capable of sustaining it, deserving of recognition. It was part of the armoury of the struggle for independence.

The leadership might thus enlist the support of those who supported the concept of independence in the metropolitan country. It might also enlist the support of other states, including the super-powers, the US and the USSR, each with its concept of a world of states and its concept of democracy. It might enlist the support of the growing number of independent states, each of them aspiring to a participatory form of government. In the course of enlisting such support, the elite was likely to find itself committed to a democratic approach. It was the best argument for independence. If it was hard for others to deny, they could not themselves deny it.

Nor when independence was secured could the elite abandon it. No independent state emerged without at least the trappings of Western-style participation. That, of course, still left the elite a great deal of flexibility, for the legacy of the West was far from unambiguous. It was possible to look to the political philosophies of the Germans, not merely of the Americans, the English, or the French, let alone the Russians, to look to corporatism as well as Communism. It was possible also to interpret the legacy of the Asian past to justify a different approach. But rarely was the concept itself abandoned. Parties, elections, assemblies had become part of the fabric of states in a world of states.

In Indonesia the preparations for independence began in the latter months of Japanese rule, some months after Koiso's pronouncement. The structures the elite envisaged reflected the authoritarian approach of the Japanese and borrowed from the Germans. Even so they recognised the need to acknowledge participation: those states after all emphasised mobilising the people, by contrast to the colonial regimes. The Japanese defeat, and the victory of the Allies, shifted that mobilisation in a more democratic direction. Adopting the trappings of democracy might win the independence movement support from the Allies. Even those who had no strong belief in Western democracy saw the strategic value of this approach. Those who believed in it, however, assumed a bolder political role, like Sjahrir. A republic that seemed not only stable and in command but also democratic in stance might win the support of the Americans. It was an argument against the return of the colonial power. No elections were held in Indonesia until 1955, but a parliamentary system was set up, and a single party pattern was replaced by a multi-party one.

What effect that had on the winning of independence is a matter for debate. Arguably it enabled the Indonesians to win support in other states and, inasmuch as that was crucial for securing independence, the adoption of the political system was justified. It might also be argued that a more unified approach would have enhanced the resistance to the Dutch forces in Indonesia, though that may in the end have been insufficient on its own. It was necessary to balance between two strategies for independence, rather than adopt one or the other. The need to resist the Dutch after all helped to promote a wide measure of unity among Republicans that survived the political struggles and limited them. Crucially that unity also survived the attempted Communist coup of 1948. And once again that helped the Indonesians win international support, that of the US in the new conditions of the Cold War. The question was whether such a degree of consensus would in turn survive the defeat of the Dutch.

In the meantime the democratic approach appeared, rightly or wrongly, to be associated with the winning of independence. It was also, with Indonesia as with other states at that time, seen as a mark of maturity, alongside recognition by other states and acceptance as a member of the UN. After 1949 the Indonesians felt bound to fulfil the democratic programme. So far parliament had been appointed. Somewhat reluctantly, its members prepared the way for elections, held in 1955. In one way, they were a triumph. The involvement of the Indonesian masses was quite remarkable. Whatever it was they made of the process, they turned out in a way that could shame other states allegedly experienced in democracy twice in one year, to vote in elections first for a parliament, then for a constituent assembly. The drawback of the elections was not only that they revealed divisions among Indonesians but that they consolidated them into representation by four major parties. Moreover minority and mediatory elements, which had been represented in the appointed parliament, were squeezed out of the elected one. Those who had never believed Western democracy would work attacked the system. The President, a leading critic, advocated, however, a different kind of democracy, rather than no democracy at all. 'I am not a managing director of the Indonesian republic and I don't want to become a dictator because it is contrary to my conscience. I am a democrat. But I don't desire democratic liberalism. On the contrary I want a guided democracy...'[5]

In Vietnam the quest for independence and the insistence on democracy were closely associated by the Viet-minh. Again it was, of course, part of a strategy for enlisting American support over against the returning colonial power. In 1945 Ho Chi Minh and his colleagues explicitly referred to the

American declaration of independence. '"All men are created equal. They are endowed by their Creator with certain unalienable rights..."' Now, the declaration of 2 September went on, 'if we enlarge the sphere of our thoughts, this statement conveys another meaning: All the peoples have a right to live, be happy and free'.[6] The sincerity with which the idea was held might be limited: the concept would certainly be perceived in a way that differed from that of the Americans. The words still meant something. In particular they implied a commitment to participation that was new to Vietnam as it was to most of Southeast Asia. One of the most significant legacies of colonialism was something that it had itself often been reluctant to accept and that it could hardly implement.

The British in prewar Burma had gone further down the track than the other European colonial powers, at least so far as the Burman peoples were concerned. What Governor Dorman-Smith and the AFPFL differed about in 1945–6 was the nature of participation. At the end of a war against totalitarianism, neither the governor, nor indeed his superiors, were ready to accept what they saw as a one-party regime. Burma must develop 'in an orderly way; and it would be contrary to the true interests of the country that a particular programme should be imposed through the rapid seizing of power by one group'.[7] Aung San and his colleagues, by contrast, saw British policy as divisive. Mountbatten backed them. Dealing with AFPFL was the best option in the long as well as the short term, he believed, a one-party state though it might favour.

Something of the same paradox affected American policy in the Philippines. Republicans and Democrats had agreed that it was headed for independence. The Republicans had, however, been less anxious to speed the process and opposed fixing a date. They argued that the Philippines was not ready and that early independence would consolidate the tendency to rule by the few. It would, Taft had declared, 'subject the great mass of their people to the dominance of an oligarchical and, probably, exploiting minority'.[8] There was much in their view, though, to set against it. There was the perennial question: could independence be prepared for by limited participation? Their view did not prevail. The system remained oligarchical, at times perhaps almost totalitarian, too. 'Our President has more power than Mussolini', General Paulino Santos, an admirer of Quezon, declared.[9] But the commitment to democracy remained, whatever meaning might be attached to it from time to time.

Neither in Burma nor in the Philippines did the democratic system provide effectively for the minorities. A strong point with colonial systems, that is indeed a difficulty participatory regimes often share. Democratic rule is likely to be majority rule, and minorities are sure to be apprehensive of the impact of government decisions by a majority government. Federal systems can provide an answer. But they may not be readily accepted by the majority, particularly if they are associated with colonial powers and their divisiveness. Federalism was unacceptable in Indonesia because it was associated with the Dutch during the struggle for independence. The British had made what one official called undertakings that were 'very nearly mutually incompatible' in 1945, when promising self-government to Burmese Burma and a special regime to the Frontier Areas.[10]

Malaya perhaps provides an exception. The colonial power held out the prospect of elections as a stage in the advance to independence. After the Kuala Lumpur elections of 1952, majority Malays worked with the Chinese and the Indians in an alliance designed to win the national elections and persuade the colonial power that independence was feasible and indeed inevitable.

Siam had not known colonial rule. Its commitment to participation arose not from a search for independence, but from the promoters' coup of 1932. That indeed precipitated rule by the few, and King Prajadhipok was to criticise the weakness of their commitment to democracy. Indeed it was his argument for abdication. 'Now that I see that my desire that the people have a real voice in the affairs of the country has not been fulfilled, and as I feel that there is no longer any way for me to assist and protect the people I therefore desire to abdicate and leave my position as king from this time...'[11] The idea had, however, taken root, in Siam/Thailand as elsewhere. It was part of being a modern state. Some states had to attain modernity by overthrowing colonial rule. Siam/Thailand sought it by overthrowing an absolute monarchy that had often behaved like a colonial power, if only the better to resist colonial powers. ●

---

1   Sukarno, quoted T. Friend, *The Blue-eyed Enemy*, Princeton: Princeton University Press, 1988, p. 110.

2   quoted Lewis E. Gleeck, 'President Hoover and the Philippines', *Bulletin of the American Historical Collection*, IX, 4 (37) (October–December, 1981), p. 39. Cf Romeo V. Cruz, *America's Colonial Desk and the Philippines*, Quezon City: University of the Philippines Press, 1974, pp. 131–2.

3   Robert H. Taylor, 'The Relationship between Burmese Social Classes and British-Indian Policy on the behavior of the Burmese political elite, 1937–1942', PhD thesis, Cornell University, p. 207.

4   Hansard 443, HofC, 5/11/47, column 1884.

5   quoted J. D. Legge, *Sukarno*, London: Penguin, 1972, p. 280.

6   quoted Allan B. Cole, *Conflict in Indo-China*, Ithaca, NY: Cornell University Press, 1956, p. 19.

7   *Times*, 2 June 1945.

8   quoted G. A. Grunder and W. E. Livezey, *The Philippines and the U.S,* Norman: Oklahoma University Press, 1951, p. 101.

9   quoted Aruna Gopinath, *Manuel L. Quezon, the tutelary democrat,* Quezon City: New Day, 1987, p. 46.

10 Minute by Walsh-Atkins, 17.2.47. M/4/2811, India Office Records.

11 quoted B. A. Batson, *The End of the Absolute Monarchy in Siam,* Singapore: Oxford University Press, 1984, p. 317.

INTERNATIONAL FACTORS IN THE WINNING OF INDEPENDENCE

Ferdinand Blumentritt, Rizal's friend and admirer, wrote to him wisely of the prospects for the independence of the Philippines. 'Whenever a people have risen against another people that ruled them, a colony against the metropolis, the revolution has never succeeded on its own strength'.[1] Was independence possible to gain and sustain in a part of the world where imperialism prevailed? Rizal's revolutionary-minded successors indeed found that it was not. Their brave attempt to found a republic collapsed. No states would recognise it. One imperial state sold the country to another. And that put down resistance by a potent version of the normal imperialist mixture of force and cooptation. Fifty years later the Philippines secured its independence, and other former colonial territories in Southeast Asia were to follow. To what extent was that due to international factors? To what extent was it due to revolutionary struggles? How were they combined?

The international factors themselves may be categorised in two ways: there are states with independent status; there are states far more powerful than others. Blumentritt's remark suggests the importance to the gaining of independence by one state of the existence of independence on the part of others. In the 1890s there was a precedent for Philippines independence in the independence won by and accorded to the post-colonial Latin American states earlier in the century. But that was not seen clearly to apply in Asia. There the Indian Congress had been founded in 1885. But the British conquest of Burma had only recently been completed, and the French acquisition of Laos was more recent still. In the 1940s an Indian Dominion was able to support the Indonesian cause. And the Australians decided they should do so, too. Moreover in the 1940s, and still more in the 1950s, international forums were available for discussing and advancing the cause of independent nations.

It is, however, hard to deny that the other category of international actors played a more significant role, though it was not uninfluenced by the existence of nationalism or putative nation-states, by the presence of lesser actors on the stage, nor, indeed, by the presence of nationalist agents, exiles, and sympathisers. The Japanese incursion destroyed the hold of the imperial powers, France first by pressure then by coup, the US, Britain, the Netherlands by invasion. Once destroyed, it would be impossible, as the French had foreseen, to restore it. They must attempt, as Chauvel of the French Foreign Office put it, 'at all costs to stay in Indochina. They feel that once they are forced out of the colony their chances of ever regaining possession ... would be slim indeed.'[2] A pattern of collaboration, combined with a minimum but decisive deployment of force, would have been hard to restore. The division among the imperialists would have given the nationalists too great an opportunity. Indeed the Japanese, as defeat threatened them, set up additional obstacles to the return of the other imperialists by extending a programme of independence, already applied to Burma and the Philippines, to the Netherlands Indies also.

The role of the imperial powers after the defeat of the Japanese is less obvious, but needs analysis. Their relative strength is one factor, their aspirations another. Their priorities differed, and they shifted over time. The gaining of independence by Southeast Asian countries was deeply affected by contingent relationships with these factors. Much was, as a result, to depend on the judgments made by Southeast Asian leaders, and their ability to sustain their leadership. That is, of course, another context in which to consider the revolutionary element in the winning of independence.

Initially the super-powers were important for what they did not do as well as for what they did. Neither the US nor the Soviet Union accorded Southeast Asia a high priority in their policy-making at the end of the war. As a result, British initiatives were all the more important. Britain's policy-makers were conscious, however, of the need to shape a policy that took account both of the super-powers and of the vacuum that their approach might leave. They recognised that the old imperialism – with which they had been so much associated – could not be revived. They believed, however, that it should be succeeded by a new relationship between East and West and a new relationship between metropolis and dependency. These prospects they saw in world-wide terms, in regional terms and in territorial terms. World-wide it would give Britain a continued world role: indeed, to avoid the conflict of the super-powers in the post-colonial world seemed to require such a role. At the same time, the role would differ from region to region and from territory to territory.

In Southeast Asia Britain had its own special interests, in the resources of Malaya, in the strategic significance of Singapore. But its main emphasis was on coming to terms with nationalism. That would pre-empt the prospect of

Communist dominance, of which the British had a long-standing apprehension: 'there had been a long tradition of anti-communist policing in South and South-East Asia'.[3] At the same time, it would give them a role which might to some extent be independent of the Americans. It did, however, require the other European powers to see the prospects in their territories in the same way, particularly as the British were closely connected with them in Europe. The British were not able to persuade them to do so. As their own position deteriorated, they sought American and Commonwealth support in a more determined fashion. The onset of the Cold War meant that it was more forthcoming. The Americans had objectives of their own. So, however, did the Commonwealth partners, and that gave the British a measure of leverage with the Americans.

The Philippines was the first Southeast Asian country to gain independence, just as it had been the first to seek it. But being first was not necessarily advantageous. The independence of the new republic was accompanied by constraints and conditions required by the metropolitan power that other countries were to avoid (or cast aside) on gaining independence. There were no precedents to use against them. But it was also true that the members of the elite of the Philippines were at best ambiguous in their attitude, not only to the conditions and the constraints, but even to independence itself. It certainly seems that the Philippines gained its independence when it did as a result of an American determination to stick to its programme and to demonstrate to others its commitment to decolonisation. The limited independence that emerged, however, was not, in the event, a very convincing example. 'The country is certainly less independent than the British Dominions now are or than India will shortly become', L. H. Foulds of the British Foreign Office wrote in November 1946.[4]

Ever since the Americans took over in the Philippines, they had envisaged independence: that was the somewhat ironic rationale developed to justify an anti-imperialist power in becoming an imperial one. Americans were divided over 'when' rather than 'whether'. Republicans tended to argue that a period of preparation was needed, since an early independence would merely perpetuate the dominance of the oligarchy. Democrats, though aware of this irony, were ready to see the cause of independence advanced. The Jones Act of 1916 committed the US to grant it when the Philippines were ready. Fixing a date was not in the event the result of ideological commitment. New legislation was pushed through as a result of the depression and the concern of American sugar producers over Philippines competition. The Hare-Hawes-Cutting Act set up a Commonwealth, with an elected president but without full independence. That was scheduled after ten years of further preparation; 1946 was the due date. The US was, no doubt, made more determined to implement it, rather than less, by its defeat meanwhile at the hands of the Japanese. It would be a sign of its victory.

The attitudes of the elite had been shaped by these policies, though its members had also helped to shape them. The introduction of an electoral system on a national basis intensified their hold on politics, and also meant that they had to advocate independence, since no other political programme could outbid its electoral appeal. At the same time, they were nervous about its consequences for themselves and for their country. Their own ties to the US were intensified by the economic opportunities it offered them: even as the Americans looked towards political independence for their new colony, their policies before the depression tied it more closely to the metropolitan market. Destruction of those markets might undermine Philippines society and open the islands to intervention. Japan had acquired Taiwan in 1895, and its increased power and ambition after the First World War was a source of apprehension. Manchuria only increased that. The elite advocated independence, but it was better to advocate it than gain it. Quezon and his colleagues were nervous about the Hare-Hawes-Cutting legislation. He even sought to join the British Commonwealth. 'The prospect of receiving a new Dominion into the fold will no doubt warm the cockles of the D[ominion] O[ffice]'s heart', wrote Robert Craigie at the Foreign Office, '– but such a liability would cause less enthusiasm amongst the Service Departments.'[5]

In 1943 the Japanese offered independence within the sphere. That only made it more difficult for the victorious Americans not to stick to their programme, or for Filipinos to argue for a delay. Some of the constraints were likely to be more or less readily accepted by an elite still concerned with the markets in the US, and rightly uncertain about security in a postwar world, even though Japan had been defeated. But the US drove a hard bargain: once again interest overcame idealism, not only in respect of military bases but in respect of economic advantage.

Independence in the Philippines may not have been an example to others. Even if the Americans had been more generous, the example they set in their own dependency was superfluous. Other metropolitan powers were aware of the attitude of the Americans. Other Southeast Asian peoples were not only anxious for independence but believed that the Americans might have a role in assisting them to secure it. That was true of the Indonesians. But other states and would-be states were also important to their cause.

The struggle with the Dutch was, of course, an important feature of the Indonesian revolution. It was not merely a matter of amour propre for the Indonesians: they had to fight for their independence. Involving other powers, however, also helped them to achieve it. To interpret the story of the winning of independence involves weighing both factors and assessing their interconnexion. To contemporaries, of course, the contention presented itself as between *perdjuangan* (struggle) and *diplomasi* (diplomacy). The Indonesians often saw these as rival solutions. What brought success, perhaps, was interrelating the two, partly by design, partly by accident. The struggle with the Dutch on the ground helped to bring about their defeat. The mixture of struggle and diplomacy brought success on the international front, which completed the discomfiture of the Dutch.

In some sense the Indonesians contrived to reverse the policies the Dutch had followed in the colonial period. The Dutch had disposed of limited force, and they had aimed to maximise its effect by using it to back a complex of relationships with a divided Indonesian people. It was important for the Dutch to avoid or put an end to the international relationships the Indonesians might pursue, and in that lay the most important contribution that their otherwise rather humiliating relationship with the British made to the establishment and preservation of their power. Indonesian nationalists had seen prewar the need to reduce divisions among themselves as a means of confronting the colonial power more effectively. But they had not been able to internationalise their cause.

Now they had that opportunity, and they used it effectively. The Dutch attempted to turn to account the divisions among the Indonesians. But they had no real way of countering the internationalisation of the issue. Even had their governments enjoyed more political flexibility at home, it is hard to see how they could have effectively countered the appeal the Indonesians made in the postwar world. The challenge of the Communists, which came to alarm the Americans, only prompted them to endorse the Indonesian cause, and put pressure on the Dutch. The Dutch failed to use the Communist threat as an effective argument in their favour. Their resort to force, however, had undermined more Western-style moderates like Sjahrir. In the nationalist phase force could not develop or sustain a collaborative framework as it had in the colonial phase.

The Indonesians were indeed divided, and apparently in no better state to pursue a coherent policy than the Dutch themselves. But even their divisions could be turned to account. At the end of the war, they were faced with the defeat of the Japanese, the arrival of the British forces, the prospect of the return of the Dutch, the possible sympathy of the Americans, the less expected sympathy of the Australians and of the less independent Indians. What was important was to play the others off against the Dutch. At the outset, therefore, it was important that the republic should demonstrate that it was in command, moderate, stable, and that indeed there was no call for the return of the Dutch. It must detach itself from its Japanese origins and from the taint of collaboration, and it must not identify itself with social revolution. At the same time it should hint that negotiation was the best answer. Worse might befall if the Allies did not accept the new regime. The objectives were brilliantly achieved. The disorder was sufficient, but sufficiently controlled, to encourage negotiation. Struggle backed diplomacy, not only by what it did, but by what it threatened. Tan Malaka aptly spoke of a 'fighting diplomacy'.[6]

The British were not unresponsive. Not only was their commander, General Christison, ready to accept the cooperation of the republic, they were also concerned to avoid conflict between their largely Indian forces and the Indonesian nationalists, since that was likely to react upon the position of the army in India and their chances of retaining a military framework there that would allow them to programme India's advance to independence. At the same time they did, as ever, recognise that the Dutch were important to them in Europe as well as in Asia, and they had obligations to their allies. Uneasily committed to the Dutch, but concerned to avoid conflict in the Indies, the British sought to promote a negotiated settlement before they withdrew their forces. That, they hoped, might set the Dutch relationship with the Indonesians on a progressive path, reconciling East and West in the post-imperial phase in ways that they hoped to see replicated throughout the region. The climax of their endeavours was the Linggadjati agreement of November 1946.

The failure of the agreement was marked by the first Dutch police action in July 1947. That, John Street commented at the Foreign Office in London, was 'basically stupid'. The Dutch would lose far more by it than 'by trying to be patient and limiting their demands to what an Indonesian coalition would accept'. It was also problematic for Britain. 'We shall be in the embarrassing position of trying to follow an uneasy compromise between our position vis-a-vis South East Asia and our desire not to split Western Europe...'[7] The police action prompted more vigorous policies from the Australians, the Indians, and more importantly, the Americans. But it was the impact of the Madiun coup that led the Americans to exert real pressure on the Dutch to come to terms with the republic. In the context of the CCP's approaching triumph, as well as their growing perception of a world-wide threat from Communism, the Americans were impressed by the success of the Sukarno-Hatta nationalist leadership in dealing with Musso and Sjarifuddin. The cleavage between nationalists and Communist sympathisers was 'most welcome..., affording prospect Communist threat Indonesia would be isolated and disposed of at favourable stage in process creation sovereign Indonesia'. The moderates could be offered no quid pro quo, but the State Department 'would necessarily reconsider desirability press Dutch for conciliatory attitude towards Repub and acceptance draft agreement should Repub compromise on Communist issue'.[8] The second Dutch police action in December 1948 seemed a real threat. Instead of installing a more moderate government, it might only displace those who had shown themselves, not only relatively moderate, but also effectively anti-Communist. The US exerted pressure on the Dutch to reach a deal.

By a mixture of struggle and diplomacy – and of some luck – the Indonesian elite had won endorsement from a major power and ensured the independence of their country. A comparison might be made with Italy. It secured its existence as a state by its own efforts, but also by the efforts of others, skilfully turned to account. If the Italians had to make Italians after making Italy, a similar problem faced Indonesians. The new state faced much division, which the Eisenhower administration was tempted to exploit,[9] but it held together. The relationship with the former colonial power, however, was bad and became worse. The regional hopes of the British were disappointed.

For the Vietnamese the opportunities were fewer, and they were not able to use the international situation so effectively. They recognised the significance of the Americans and sought to appeal to them, for example by drawing up a declaration of independence, far more elaborate than that of the Indonesians, that evoked that of 1776. But the returning British were more helpful to the French than they had been to the Dutch. That was true of the local commander in the south of Vietnam: Douglas Gracey did not behave like Christison. In any case the Viet-minh were weaker in the south, and the French were able to gain a foothold there, as they had in their original colonisation. The domestic situation in France made for an even more unconstructive policy than that of the Netherlands, but the British were able to exert less pressure on the French than the Dutch: 'the French are notoriously sensitive to intervention from outside in their affairs, and such intervention is liable to produce prejudicial and unsatisfactory results.'[10] Above all, perhaps, the French benefited from their earlier errors. Their pre-war policies had tended to throw the leadership of the nationalist movement into the hands of the Communists. They could now argue that they were defending Indo-China from Communism. As the Cold War unfolded, and the CCP approached victory, the US supported the colonial power in Indo-China in a way quite unlike that in Indonesia. A long war ensued. No doubt the French were better able to sustain one than the Dutch, and they received substantial American aid. But the chances of the kind of region-wide approach that the British had hoped for were still further diminished.

International factors were less significant in the case of postwar Burma. The Japanese war had dislodged the British, and the Burmans ensured that they never effectively regained control. But the British were also influenced by their concern over the Americans. Their policy had in part at least been designed to show their Allies that their policy was forward-looking, despite Amery's declaration that 'By Gad! Sir' he was 'not at all prepared that anyone, Yank or Chink, should poke either projecting or flat noses into the problem of the reconstruction of Burma'.[11] That the British had to alter the policy, and abandon their timetabled approach, again owed something to their anxiety over India. Pitting a largely Indian army against Burman resistance was ruled out, lest it break up the Indian army. 'There can be no objection to the use of Indian troops against dacoits or bandits...', Sir C. Auchinleck wrote, 'but political difficulties will arise if they are used to quell any political or quasi-political disturbances, particularly those professing to aim at the independence of Burma'.[12] Britain's policy was also affected by its concern about Communism, which pre-dated that of the Americans. It was better to make a deal with more moderate nationalists than drive the nationalist movement to extremes by insisting on the programme laid out in the White Paper of 1945. It was better indeed to look for a stable Burma outside the Commonwealth rather than risk destabilising it by insisting on its remaining in the Commonwealth, at that time only possible if the monarch remained the head of state. In 1947 Britain had determined to cut its losses in India, but still hoped to retain it as a Dominion. There seemed some chance that the Indians might after all accept independence on that basis. The Burmans were not prepared to do so, and the British would not modify the conditions for staying in the Commonwealth for them alone. In fact the hoped-for stability did not eventuate. Independence worsened the ethnic problems which the imperial phase had failed to resolve and may even have exacerbated. The Karens felt betrayed as well as threatened.

Independence for Malaya was at the end of the war seen as a more remote prospect. The British believed that they had to build an intercommunal Malaya first. That the union plan was dropped was partly due to international factors: Indonesia might have proved an attractive option to Malay extremists. The abandonment of the union for the federation was followed by 'the emergency', so described partly in order to stress its internal character, but in fact also seen as part of an international Communist threat.[13] That was resolved not only by force, more thoroughly as well as more subtly deployed than that used by the Dutch in Indonesia or by the French and Americans in Vietnam, but also by political change. Malaya took the path to independence far more quickly than had been anticipated.

International factors could also work against independence. That was the case in Vietnam. It was also the case in Borneo. No one believed in the 1950s, for example, that Sarawak could be an independent state. It was too small to survive in an insecure world. The same was true, it seemed, of Singapore. Malaya became Malaysia. In the event Singapore was soon to become completely independent, and triumphantly so, but Sarawak, and Sabah, remained part of the new federation. Indonesian antagonism had helped to consolidate their relations with the peninsula in the early days of the new federation. ●

---

1   quoted L. M. Guerrero, *The First Filipino*, Manila: National Heroes Commission, 1963, pp. 311–12.

2   Leahy/Hull, 1/3/41, 256. FRUS 1941 V, p. 100.

3   Rolf Tanner, *A Strong Showing*, Stuttgart: Steiner, 1994, p. 144.

4   Memo in Foulds/Bevin, 21/11/46, 94. FO371/34344 [F17690/10035/83].

5   Minute, 1 November 1933. FO371/16611 [A 7649/89/45].

6   R. Mrázek, *Sjahrir. Politics and Exile in Indonesia*, Ithaca: Southeast Asia Program, Cornell University, 1994, p. 308.

7   Minute, 21/7/47. FO371/63605 [F9759/45/62].

8   Ag SofS/CG, 27/9/48, Cable 449. FRUS 1948 VI, pp. 378–9.

9   Audrey R. and George McT. Kahin, *Subversion as Foreign Policy*, New York: The New Press, 1995, pp. 87ff.

10 Minute by Allen, 21/12/46. FO371/53969 [F18076/8/61].

11 Amery/Dorman-Smith, 29/12/42. Eur.E. 215/2, India Office Library.

12 CinC India/SACSEA, 18/10/45. M/5/91, India Office Library.

13 cf Richard Stubbs, *Hearts and Minds in Guerrilla Warfare*, Singapore: Oxford University Press, 1989, pp. 66–9.

ARMIES

The 'Western' image of the army is of the kind of force that emerged with the modern European state. The army's role was to defend that state from its external enemies, who might or might be thought to be threatening it. Its role within the state was largely associated with its role outside the state. At times, indeed, it might be called upon to deal with domestic crises or with internal unrest. For the most part, however, its focus was outwards. That could, of course, be useful domestically. A regime might win support at home by concentrating on enemies abroad, and the army might win a corresponding influence at home, and a corresponding share of the budget. But such were more likely to be the effects of international crisis, which would affect democratic as well as authoritarian regimes. The role of the army within states would change because the relationships among states changed.

In some sense the colonial world was insulated from this process. Before the colonial powers arrived, Southeast Asia had, of course, known intra-regional conflict, sometimes on a large and indeed devastating scale, in particular, perhaps, in respect of the conflicts between Burma and Siam. The establishment of the colonial powers was often marked by bursts of violence, sometimes succeeded by periods of guerilla warfare, as again in Burma, and in Vietnam, too, and on American entry into the Philippines. But once that authority was established, military conflict diminished. In a perhaps unprecedented way, Southeast Asian societies were demilitarised. Insofar as the colonial powers used force, and did not rely on coopting elites, they used it on as limited a scale as possible. Its deployment was intended to back up a political structure, not replace it. Occasional bursts of terror were designed to reduce the overall use of force not increase it.

The colonial armies, often drawn from minority peoples, or from colonial territories other than the one in hand, were more like armed constabularies than armies. They were not designed to defend the territory from its neighbours. That was ensured by the relationships of the powers elsewhere, in Europe above all, and later in East Asia. The territories were protected, too, by the disposition of naval forces. They were, thirdly, protected by the predominance of the British throughout the nineteenth century, joined as a status quo power by the Americans in the twentieth. When these defences failed, the territories were without defence. It was difficult to develop armies to defend the territories at so late a date. It was indeed not clear that, in the absence of a sense of identification with the colonial power, armies could have been raised that would have fought for the status quo. There was a sense in which the colonial regimes must fall if they could not defend themselves. To elicit loyalty they would have to behave like the independent states they could not in fact be. Even the strongest of the colonial powers generally shrank from raising national armies. Such an army, recruited from the majority people, might render the continuance of colonial rule impossible.

The winning of independence implied that armies in Southeast Asia must expect to be different and to assume a different role. The territories became states in a world of states, and in a world of states the armed forces must become defence forces rather than mere constabularies. But if there was a change in principle, the change in practice was a slower process. For one thing, the new states emerged from fragments of empire, and the armies were given, or assumed, a large role in nation-building. At the same time, the international situation, full of tension among the great powers, tended to preserve the integrity of the small ones. Conflict among them, though not unprecedented, occurred but rarely. The Cold War world was a post-colonial one. Only with the end of the Cold War did a new kind of uncertainty emerge. Then the Southeast Asian states, pressed by new security concerns, as well as by the established interests of their armed services, began to arm more determinedly while at the same time seeking a regional consensus as a sanction for the status quo.

The armies of post-colonial Southeast Asia reflected this sequence of changes in their structure, in their perception of their role, in their recruitment, in their size, in their armaments. But often the armies retained substantial internal functions, and indeed augmented them by involvement in development. Distinguishing it from the 'professionalism' of earlier armies, that augmentation is sometimes captured in, if not rationalised by, the term 'new professionalism'.[1]

The Indonesian army was put together from a number of sources that reflect the stages of development in the state itself. Some of its officer elite was drawn from the KNIL, the Dutch-recruited army of the colonial period, recruited from the majority people of the Indies, the Javanese, but characteristically from a range of others (in 1937 it included 12,700 Javanese, 5,100 Menadonese, 4,000 Ambonese, 1,800 Sundanese, 1,100 Timorese, and 400 Madurese, Bugis, Acehnese, and Malays).[2] Others, more often Javanese, came from the Japanese-period army, the PETA. Yet others were drawn from the guerilla forces that were mobilised against the return of the Dutch. Creating an army for the republic out of these disparate component parts was a difficult task, especially if it were to be modernised, better armed, and thus reduced in size. The army indeed reflected the divisions of Indonesia in the 1950s more than it resolved them. That no doubt helped to restrain it from taking power itself, though it had, since the struggle against the Dutch, seen itself as a special guardian of the state. Sukarno's proclamation of martial law and Suharto's take-over opened up wider opportunities for the military. They not only helped to consolidate the army. They also rooted it more deeply in civil society. Though powerful, and indeed predominant within Indonesia, it was still focused on internal affairs. The largest state in Southeast Asia concentrated its force on maintaining its unity rather than on asserting its regional predominance by other than diplomatic means. In so doing, of course, it provoked other tensions within the state, and diminished the options for resolving them. The *dwifungsi* concept suggests that civilian and military authorities are both involved in security, both involved in development. The concept is widely accepted, though its interpretation may be questioned.[3]

The Burman army offers some parallels. Its initial leaders came partly from the BDA of the Japanese phase, partly from the British-trained minority forces. Its role was strengthened by the near-disaster that followed independence, though it also polarised the relationships of Burmans and minority groups. The army seized power in 1962 and has never relinquished it since. Again, however, it is an army concerned with its own interests and with holding the state together, in this case as a Burman-dominated union, and upholding an authoritarian, as against a democratic, approach.

The role of the army in the Philippines was far less prominent before the advent of Ferdinand Marcos as president in 1965. 'Marcos characterized the military in various terms like: "catalyst of social change", a "training institution for national leaders", the "defender of the seat of government", a "nation builder", and a "model of national discipline and self reliance".'[4] Even before Marcos, however, it had begun to undertake 'civic action' tasks that were not seen as an army's in Western countries. Often that was considered worthwhile and justified. It was not merely that it had to deal with the Huk guerillas. Should not an army that has no substantial role in defence use its trained personnel and its equipment in worthwhile civic action? The risk was, of course, the politicisation of the army. Of that there had already been some. But what may have been acceptable under Magsaysay and Macapagal became an abuse under Marcos. The army's share of power and of the budget vastly expanded.

The case of Vietnam is different again. There, of course, the Communist-led nationalist movement engaged in a long struggle with the metropolitan power. That was followed by a long struggle with a super-power, the US. That power also endeavoured to sustain a South Vietnamese state and to enable that state to fight with its own power. The endeavour collapsed, and Vietnam became independent under the Communists. In postwar Vietnam, not unnaturally army officers had a large role. The impact of the changes in the Soviet Union on the Seventh Party Congress in 1991 indeed prompted an increase in military influence. 'This heavy concentration of military men is likely to find reflection in opposition not only to cuts in the size of the armed forces but to any move towards greater pluralism or multi-party democracy.'[5]

Though army officers are powerful there, too, Thailand also differs. It never fell under colonial rule. No more did it fight a major power, apart from its tussle with Vichy France in 1941, its mild resistance to the Japanese later that year, and its formal declarations of war on the UK and the US early in 1942. The army had, however, secured a prominent role after the 1932 coup, increasingly, indeed, a dominant role. Despite the democratic ideals of some of the Promoters, Thailand was a bureaucratic state. In many ways the army was itself a bureaucratic structure. 'Politics is government service and government service is politics... If the military is also responsible for government service, how can it be separated from politics?' General Arthit Kamlang-ek asked.[6] Greatly strengthened when Thailand was seen as a bastion against the Communists, the army still did not focus on conflict outside the borders of the state, but on manipulating conflict within it. Parliamentary Thailand has to accommodate it and accommodate to it.

The armies of Southeast Asia indeed remained in the post-colonial period armies devoted to sustaining authority within the frontiers – sometimes their own as much as the government's – more than to providing for their defence from outside attack; still less were they designed for aggression against their neighbours. The elements of which they were made up had changed. Their size had grown. They had different political roles. But they were above all still constabularies. Such a stance was likely to shift in the post-Cold War world. A constabulary role might still be required in several countries, but Southeast Asian states would generally need to enhance their defence capacity. Their disposition was, however, to collaborate, not by formal alliance, but through a network of regional relationships, personal and organisational.

It might indeed prove that other elements in the armed forces would undergo greater change than the armies. The colonial status quo had been sustained over against other powers by naval more than by military strength, in particular by that of the British. The post-colonial order was sustained in substantial part by the positioning of the US 7th Fleet. Building a navy is a task still lying ahead for most of the Southeast Asian states, though island Indonesia had long been aware of the need, and controversially sought an instant increment of naval power in the sell-off by East Germany. Navy-building may affect relationships within Southeast Asia. But, again, the region as a whole must take account of the naval plans of the major powers, above all the People's Republic of China.

British power was overthrown not only by military and naval attack but by attack from the air. It may indeed be in the air that the defence concerns of the independent Southeast Asian states are most clearly demonstrated. Thailand and Malaysia appear to see their air forces as deterrent. But again there are elements of collaboration across the region.

Within the regional framework, the smallest states may still have particular concerns. A small and wealthy state with a population mainly Chinese in origin, Singapore has decided to demonstrate that it will not be easy to eliminate. Some of its closest military contacts have been with Israel. A Muslim state, Brunei is even smaller and even wealthier. It, too, can afford armed forces, the purpose of which is mainly deterrent.

---

1   quoted J. Soedjati Djiwandono and Yong Mun Cheong, eds, *Soldiers and Stability in Southeast Asia*, Singapore, ISEAS, 1988, p 17

2   H. L. Zwitzer en C. A. Heshusius, *Het Koninklijk Nederlands-Indisch Leger 1830–1950*, The Hague: Staatuitgeverij, 1977, p. 10.

3   Salim Said, *Genesis of Power*, Singapore: ISEAS, 1991, p. 142.

4   A. F. Celoza, 'The Rise of an Authoritarian Regime in the Philippines', PhD thesis, Claremont Graduate School, 1987, p. 252.

5   Michael C. Williams, *Vietnam at the Cross roads*, New York: Council on Foreign Relations Press, 1992, p. 37.

6   quoted Soedjati and Yong, p. 23.

MILLENARIANISM

There has been much excellent historical writing about millennialism, messianism and millenarianism in Southeast Asia. Some of it has been partly or wholly theoretical in nature. Sartono Kartodirdjo's *Peasant Movements in Rural Java*, for example, makes a useful attempt to define and categorise.[1] Other works have been more narrative in style, while still being analytical in character. Sartono's own *The Peasant Revolt in Banten in 1888* is an example of this genre.[2] In *Pasyon and Revolution*, Reynaldo Ileto has expanded our understanding of the Philippines revolution by relating peasant involvement to the millenarian promise implied by translating the Christian message of resurrection to this world.[3] In his *Prophets of Rebellion: millenarian protest movements against the European colonial order*, Michael Adas has described peasant unrest in Burma,[4] and Hue-Tam Ho Tai has written of *Millenarianism and Peasant Politics in Vietnam*.[5] The topic has fascinated historians and students, and it is complementary to several of the central topics of the present book.

Some questions arise as a result of a focus on Southeast Asia. Are such movements peculiar to that region? Are they peculiar to a colonial world? The answer to both questions is negative. Elsewhere in Asia millenarianism is well recognised in peasant history. The Little Tradition in China comprises a strong element of it, and so do the *yonaoshi* or 'world renewal' movements in Japan.[6] Nor, as these cases suggest, is the movement confined to colonial countries. Indeed millennial attitudes are familiar in European societies, too, particularly (though not exclusively) in peasant societies. Sartono's movements mostly belong to colonial Java, but it seems likely that this is because the records for that period reveal more evidence, rather than because such movements did not exist before the Dutch arrived. Certainly they existed in most peasant societies, and the spirit is not dead even in more sophisticated societies.

What the movements have in common is not a colonial experience: it is an experience of a non-participatory polity. Often such movements arise at a time of change, and its adverse results provoke a wish to recapture an apparently better past or to pre-empt a happier future, or both. Those who participate are clear that change cannot be effected in any other way than by inspired action, by trust, by faith, by following a charismatic leader, by a kind of magic. It is not satisfactory to regard it merely as an irrational approach, but it does not follow the rationality of political participation. That is not available, or not seen to be available.

In a colonial structure that, of course, is a likely state of affairs. There can be little sense that change can be brought about by political action of a 'modern' kind if the rulers are demonstrably of another race and backed by outside power. But the state of affairs is not peculiar to a colonial structure. There was little sense that change could be brought about, or reversed, in China or in Japan. In Europe itself, after all, Marx had to contend with utopianism. That, he believed, was indeed a main enemy. It conduced to action that was bound to be ineffectual, revolutions that were certain to be disappointed. He urged what he called a 'scientific' approach, that took account of historical trends and practical realities. Even he retained a residue of utopianism. 'He had simply thrust the happy consummation a little farther off into the future.'[7]

Marxist activists had to work their way through this contradiction. The most successful were those who insisted on patient political work, indoctrination, organisation, coupled with planned violence, and discounted rapid results. Mao had to oppose the adventurism of Li Li San. Ho had to organise the Vietnam Communist Party after the disasters of the 1930s. The Indonesian party had perhaps the most chequered history of all. It was the oldest in Asia, but one of the least successful. The strain of millenialism it picked up in Indonesia it failed to counter by patient political work. More than once it acted prematurely. More than once, it was virtually destroyed as a result: in 1926–7, in 1948, in 1965.

Indonesian Communism had an early start, as a result of the contacts with the Dutch Communists. In the Philippines, Communism was of much later origin, postdating not only millennialist movements, but the advent of a middle-class leadership that sought to modernise them. The millenial movements were, as Ileto has shown, deeply influenced by popular Catholicism: its promise of redemption was transferred to the world of the present and the immediate future. Most famous were the colorum sects, deriving from the movement of Apolinario de la Cruz. Even in that case there was a link between peasant unrest and middle-class leadership, since Apolinario was a disappointed secular cleric. In the 1930s the link was established in another way. Ramos, a disappointed place-holder, capitalised on peasant unrest with his Sakdal movement. But his attempts to modernise it were a failure. The ruling oligarchy was not disposed to permit much participation in politics. And the belief in invulnerability was destroyed by constabulary bullets. 'Exaltation turned to astonishment, followed quickly by blind panic.'[8] The unrest during and after the Pacific war was canalised more effectively by the Hukbalahap leaders, who indeed shared Communist ideas, though hardly attempting to create a cadre party.

Peasant unrest took more traditional forms in Burma, too. There, indeed, Communism, inhibited by British rule, was slow to take hold, and when it did, slow to attempt political work among the peasants. The Saya San uprising of 1930–1 was traditional in character, evoking the values of Buddhism and of the monarchy the British had overthrown. 'The Burman peasants in general are amazingly superstitious and extraordinarily ignorant and credulous, a fact which is well attested by the pathetic and widespread belief among those who participated in the various risings, that "tattoo marks", "charmed handkerchiefs", "embedment needles", "charmed oil", "charmed lime", "magic gong", "charmed stanzas", etc., would render them "immune to bullets and dah cuts".'[9] With the emergence of the Thakin leadership and the Japanese occupation, the Burman leaders set out to secure independence. Within that movement there were self-styled Communists and, though they were denied a share of power, the regime pursued left-wing policies. That may have limited the revival of millenialism.

The same kind of challenge faced the Communists in Vietnam. Depression, floods, the growing threat of war affected the population of Nam Bo in the 1930s. But mass movements were not enough: 'the assumptions and the aims of secular politics must be well understood if the popular base is to remain cohesive for any length of time. The cadres had to teach the peasants not only how to form committees of action and how to draw up lists of grievances and demands, but also why this type of activity was different from joining sect-organizations and participating in undirected millenarian violence.'[10]

Peasant unrest does not necessarily take the form of millenial or more or less political movements. In *The Moral Economy of the Peasant: Rebellion and subsistence in Southeast Asia* and *Weapons of the Weak: Everyday forms of peasant resistance*, James Scott had described other forms of peasant resistance, small deeds that limit the exactions of landlords, or frustrate the excesses of the powerful.[11] Nor, on the other hand, is millenial aspiration necessarily connected only with agrarian unrest. The frustration that is its characteristic origin is found in the city as well as in the countryside, as the Rizalista cults suggest.[12] The only counter is in fact an open political system, in which participation takes place and appears to achieve satisfactory results.

The people's revolution in the Philippines followed upon the repressive dictatorship Marcos had inaugurated by declaring an emergency in 1972. That had retained but emasculated democratic forms. Its overthrow in 1986 was not simply the result of a political and military coup: it was also the result of a massive popular intervention. Some of its potency derived no doubt from the millennial strand in Philippines political life: it was a rare success for popular forces. At the same time it left a legacy of expectation that the successor Aquino regime could not fulfil. In another sense, it related to

Philippines nationalism. The year 1986 seemed to be an example to other authoritarian countries, just as, in Mabini's hopes, 1896 had been 'contagious'. ●

---

1   S. Kartodirdjo, *Peasant Movements in Rural Java*, Singapore: Oxford University Press, 1973.

2   S. Kartodirdjo, *The Peasant Revolt in Banten in 1888*, The Hague: Nijhoff, 1966.

3   R. Ileto, *Pasyon and Revolution*, Quezon City: Ateneo de Manila Press, 1979.

4   M. Adas, *Prophets of Rebellion: Millenarian protest movements against the European colonial order*, Chapel Hill: University of N. Carolina Press, 1979.

5   Hue-Tam Ho Tai, *Millenarianism and Peasant Politics in Vietnam*, Cambridge, Mass.: Harvard University Press, 1983.

6   Cf George Wilson in Tetsuo Najita and J. Victor Koschmann, eds, *Conflict in Modern Japanese History*, Princeton: Princeton University Press, 1982, p. 186.

7   Edmund Wilson, *To the Finland Station*, London: Secker, n.d., p. 332.

8   David R. Sturtevant, *Popular uprisings in the Philippines*, Ithaca: Cornell University Press, 1976, p. 241.

9   *The Origin and Causes of the Burma Rebellion, 1930–32*, Rangoon, 1934, p. 43.

10 Hue-Tam Ho Tai, p. 108.

11 J. Scott, *The Moral Economy of the Peasant: Rebellion and subsistence in Southeast Asia*, New Haven: Yale University Press, 1976. J. Scott, *Weapons of the Weak: Everyday forms of peasant resistance*, New Haven: Yale University Press, 1985.

12 M. A. Foronda, *Cults Honoring Rizal*, Manila, 1961.

FOREIGN POLICY

The political entities of Southeast Asia have had various systems of interrelationship over the centuries. It would be mistaken to describe them as international relations, since that would presume that they were relationships among 'nations' or 'nation-states'. Such did not exist. Even the word 'state' may convey a mistaken sense of the reality. A more neutral term like 'political entity' may itself not be neutral enough, but it avoids some 'presentist' presumptions, and offers some means of describing the past which is itself 'another country'.

Relationships existed that reflected the relative position of such entities and allowed them to find a recognised place within a commonly conceived world. The main relationship in East Asia was that between China and its neighbours. It was one that depended on the concept of a Middle Kingdom, between heaven and earth. This was 'the mechanism by which barbarous non-Chinese regions were given their place in the all-embracing Chinese political, and therefore ethical, scheme of things'.[1] Other states, other entities, found their place in the world in relation to it according to their greater or lesser levels of civilisation and to their readiness to accept both the elements of suzerainty and vassalage and the elements of qualified mutuality on which the system rested. Like other systems of relationship among entities, it allowed for an element of make-believe. Formality had its own importance, even if it did not always conform to reality.

Indeed, the system lent itself to paradox. Some states were inclined to imitate the inimitable, and themselves to define their relationships with neighbours, and indeed with more remote states, in terms of suzerainty and vassalage. The most obvious example and the strongest paradox are found in the case of Vietnam. Seeking in internal affairs often to adopt the Chinese model, as Alexander Woodside has put it, it was tempted to adopt it for its relationship with others, too, and to list a series of dependencies in some kind of imitation of the Middle Kingdom itself. 'This meant that diplomatic intercourse with them could only be carried out at the Vietnamese court if their envoys to Hué followed the ritualized behavior of vassals.'[2]

The example of China was, however, not the only reason why the relationships between entities might be conceived in such a way. Some entities were more powerful than others, and the system afforded a means of accepting that. A confession of 'vassalage' would not only redound to the credit of the greater, but it would help to preserve the position of the weaker. It might enable a lesser entity to preserve a degree of independence of a greater. In effect, by recognising its neighbour's power, it might limit the temptation to use it. A 'de jure' acceptance of suzerainty might, to adopt European terms, avoid a 'de facto' exercise of sovereignty. The Vietnamese were adept at this. Siam itself saw fit to send missions to the Middle Kingdom until the mid-nineteenth century. In some sense it was an insurance policy.

The system also reflected the nature of the entities themselves in Southeast Asia. Characteristically the states lacked the rigid geographical frontiers of later systems. Tribute and allegiance were related to the more personal links that bound political entities together and that related rulers and peoples. Sometimes, indeed, it was possible, as it might be desirable, for a ruler to offer allegiance to more than one great neighbour. It reflected a reality in the affairs of a state like Cambodia, placed between Siam and Vietnam; of a state like Kedah, seeking to limit the exercise of Thai suzerainty and, according at least to the Thais, its ruler so thinking 'of connecting himself with the Burmese enemies, to whom he sent a man with letters'.[3] At times it could be a risky policy, rather than a reflection of reality. It was in any case a way of operating the state system of the time, a kind of diplomacy.

The advent of the colonial powers changed the system. It did not happen, of course, all at once. The elimination of the Chinese relationship was achieved only with the Franco-Chinese war of the 1880s and the negotiations between Britain and China over the frontiers of British Burma. Elsewhere in Southeast Asia, colonial powers both used and displaced the old system. It was convenient for France to assert Vietnamese claims over Cambodia and Laos. It was convenient for Britain to accept or even later to take over some of the Thai claims on the Malay Peninsula, and to modify and reject others. The Dutch might base a claim to West Irian on the claims of the Sultan of Tidore, though in the end making West New Guinea part of, indeed the last part of, their empire in the Indies.

Characteristically, however, Southeast Asia became divided among colonial powers. In substantial part, it ceased to have a system of inter-entity relations. The diplomacy that affected Southeast Asia was conducted among metropolitan powers, often indeed only as part of a wider diplomacy, and subject to the dictates of interests in other parts of the world. The relationships among the rulers of Southeast Asian territories were circumscribed. The relations of governor of the Straits Settlements and the governor of the Netherlands Indies were less important than the relationships of London and The Hague: indeed they rarely, if ever, exchanged correspondence, let alone visits.

The Thais, remaining independent, profited from the situation. They could limit their contacts with the governor of the Straits Settlements and work through the British Foreign Office's representative in Bangkok: they alone had a state that, in some sense, belonged to the world of interstate relationships that was emerging. Mongkut was delighted to receive the letter from Queen Victoria that Harry Parkes delivered in 1856: he was thus 'admitted unreservedly into the brotherhood of European royalty', and 'his position as a King thus clearly recognised by the Sovereign of the most powerful European State'.[4] Those who sought to emerge into that world realised the significance of their inability to conduct a foreign policy. Quezon was to be frustrated by the semi-independence of the Commonwealth of the Philippines: 'he could now definitely say one thing, which was that he would never recommend to his people a perpetuation of the present condition of semi-subordination'.[5] How could he prepare for the independence of the Philippines if he could not conduct foreign policy as well as enjoy domestic autonomy?

The postwar period saw the spread to Southeast Asia and then to other parts of the world of the system of nation-states and with it the system of international relations that the Europeans, and then the Americans, had been building up over a century or more. It was a system that again mixed rhetoric and reality. States were equal in sovereignty, but not in power. A state had to be 'recognised' by others and that normally was accompanied by a seat in the UN General Assembly. But in fact independence was a matter of degree. To enjoy as much of it as was possible, a state had to recognise the limits of the possible. To be independent, a state had to recognise that others were more independent. Only an acceptance that power was differentially distributed made the concept of theoretical equality viable.

Understanding the foreign policy of the emergent states, as indeed that of others, requires some such consideration of the nature of the system in which they had to work. It also requires some consideration of the aims of foreign policy in such a system of states. A state must aim first of all at security, at the preservation of its frontiers, and at a due measure of independence. It has also come to be accepted, second, that a state has to seek the prosperity of its subjects, and that diplomacy can no longer be merely concerned with political security. Third, a state may be expected to aim, in part perhaps to ensure these objectives, but in part also because of the dynamics of the system, to exert an influence in the region and in the world commensurate with its power, its size, its wealth. It is the acceptance of that, both on the part of the stronger and of the weaker, that lies at the very heart of the system. It is the moderation, the consideration, the mutual antagonism and forbearance, the reconciliation of divergent interests, that form the stuff of its diplomacy.

Understanding the foreign policy of states in a world of states requires some additions to this simple model. The model emphasises interests rather than ideologies, for example, perhaps unduly. Pursuing an ideology may support the pursuit of an interest; it may complicate it; it may even damage it. It is also likely to change the perception of a state's policy on the part of other states. Even if a state does not avowedly include an ideological formulation in its foreign policy, it may approach foreign policy in preconditioned ways. The policy-making elite may have a conception of the state that is reflected in its foreign policy. The Indonesian elite, for example, saw their republic, though the inheritor of Dutch frontiers, as born of revolution: that made it difficult to accept the validity of the creation of a Malaysian state that seemed to be born of colonialism and compromise, 'the marriage between Malay feudalism and British imperialism',[6] adding to the other challenges Malaysia seemed to represent, perhaps to Indonesia's security, certainly to its sense of itself as the regional leader.

The role of public opinion in foreign policy has long been a source of controversy. One issue is its definition. European statesmen, like the great Lord Salisbury, might refer to it, but even in parliamentary Britain, it seemed to be rather an excuse than a reason for a particular policy. Were the elite using public opinion to support a predetermined line, to avoid a commitment, for example? Certainly the involvement of public opinion, once evoked, might reduce the room for manoeuvre that a maker of foreign policy might have. The discrediting of secret diplomacy by the outbreak of the First World War led to a demand for open agreements, openly arrived at. But that was in fact impractical. Openness could only become a camouflage, if not an obstruction, to a diplomacy that has to be secret. Nor was the wisdom of the many necessarily better than the wisdom of the few in a kind of human relations that required give-and-take, negotiation, compromise.

The definition of public opinion is itself a difficult task. The easiest sources for an historian to pursue are the newspapers of the day. But newspaper readers do not necessarily share the opinions of newspaper editors or leader-writers. Other avenues have been explored in order to determine, as in Jean Jacques Becker's case, why the French went to war in 1914.[7] We know enough of Italian 'public opinion' to know why Italy should not have gone to war in 1915, and we know how a minority of the 'public' was allowed to overwhelm parliamentary opinion.

In new states, as indeed in Italy itself, a cause in foreign policy may indeed arouse public opinion even more than in old ones. Evoking a national cause may unify the nation, but there may well be a cost in foreign policy. Will it drive foreign policy beyond its rational limits? Will it prejudice its objectives, security, prosperity, an influence in the world commensurate with the possession of power? The case of *konfrontasi* is a case in point.

Indonesia had pursued a strikingly successful foreign policy ever since independence. Indeed winning independence had been part of it: it was not only a heroic military struggle, but a clever diplomatic one, in which Indonesia took account of US and 'world' opinion, of the attitudes of India and Australia, in a way that completely evaded the Dutch. The mixture of force and diplomacy, in a sense a rejigging of the combination the Dutch had themselves used in Indonesia, served them well, too, in securing West New Guinea in 1961. But it did not work when they 'confronted' Malaysia, and Indonesia was driven, by the combination of frustration and internal pressures, into an extreme policy that was unlikely to bring success abroad and likely indeed to bring division at home. *Konfrontasi* had its rational side. As the major regional state, Indonesia had a 'right' to a say in the fate of its neighbours, though how that was to be effected was unclear. But it tended to obscure its real claim to be involved by a high-pressure mix of force and diplomacy that was in the end counter-productive. It alienated world opinion, and did not win US support. And it tended to consolidate Malaysia rather than break it up. Only in the longer term might its policy be deemed to have enjoyed some kind of success. The pressure on Britain had been considerable, and it made it more likely that it would reduce its commitments in Southeast Asia in the late 1960s and 1970s, particularly as Suharto had destroyed the Communists. The way was prepared for Indonesia to pursue a regional role in a more moderate style.

The Philippines had also endeavoured to intervene in the creation of Malaysia. Its policy was again a mixture of interest and ideology. North Borneo had originally been secured partly by agreement with the Sultan of

Sulu, and now it was to change its status, perhaps finally, by becoming part of a nation-state. The sultan's heirs were interested; so indeed was the republic itself, despite the treaty its predecessor, Spain, had made with Britain in 1885. Its interest, however, was not merely economic; it was also political. In some sense Filipinos such as Mabini had seen themselves as leaders in Southeast Asia, and this aspiration to a larger role had become associated with the North Borneo claim. President Macapagal drew on this tradition. At the same time, it ought to be said, as in the West New Guinea case, the new state had some reason to be dissatisfied with the old boundary: it did not make it easier to maintain security. The foreign policy of the Philippines was a failure. Maphilindo, its achievement, was an ephemeral association: the combination of Malaya, Philippines and Indonesia did not survive.

Interest and ideology are interspersed in the foreign policies of mainland states as well. For Vietnam it was useful that the Communist great powers, China and Russia, contended: it could reduce its risk of dependence on the former by a judicious connexion with the latter. Placed between India and China, Burma pursued a policy of isolationism that could be rationalised by its position as well as by the ideology of its leaders. The changes since 1989 are challenging the approaches of both countries but also promoting relations with their Southeast Asian neighbours. ●

---

1   J. K. Fairbank and S. Y. Teng, 'On the Ch'ing Tributary System', *Harvard Journal of Asiatic Studies*, VI, 2 (June 1941), p. 139.

2   Woodside, p. 237.

3   quoted R. Bonney, *Kedah 1771–1821*, Kuala Lumpur: Oxford University Press, 1971, p. 161.

4   Parkes/Clarendon, 22/5/1856. FO 69/5.

5   Blunt/FO, 18/12/35, 103. FO371/19822 [A744/34/45].

6   quoted G. Mc T. Kahin, 'Malaysia and Indonesia', *Pacific Affairs*, 37.3 (Fall 1964), p. 261.

7   *1914, Comment les Français sont entrés dans la guerre*, Paris: Presses Universitaires, c. 1977.

Part Three

PERIODS AND PERSPECTIVES

Part One of this book sought to outline the emergence of the modern states of Southeast Asia. Part Two discussed a number of topics in their history that can be considered regionally and comparatively. Both approaches can be criticised from the perspective of a modern Western historiography. That itself is, of course, not the only perspective on the past that has been adopted in the West, nor, indeed, in Southeast Asia.

The third part of the book discusses some of the distinctive features of that historiography and some of the ways in which they have been or can be turned to account.

TIME AND PLACE

'Time has no divisions to mark its passage, there is never a thunderstorm or blare of trumpets to announce the beginning of a new month or year. Even when a new century begins it is only we mortals who ring bells and fire off pistols.'[1] We mortals differ in the way we divide up time. Those differences themselves alter over time.

In the oral environments Barbara Andaya describes in her work on Southeast Sumatra, stories were handed down from the past: they were 'ever-mutating', but 'perceived as unchanging'.[2] There was no sense of sequential time. Lucian Pye felt that 'the Burmese lack any feeling for tidiness in history; they do not see history in terms of stages or phases, and so they are not led to see one sequence rounded off before the next is begun'.[3] 'What could provide a time-referent for different groups', Barbara Andaya continued, '...was the reign of a common overlord'.[4] The lives of kings could present 'a means of identifying a shared block of time'.[5] That, of course, remained a common concept in other societies, in Europe and elsewhere, where there was a greater sense of the passage of time. One lived in Good King Charles' Golden Days or in the Meiji era.

Such a view of the passage of time sometimes had, both in Asian and European societies, another dimension: the concept of decline and restoration. It suggested that change was neither evolutionary nor, except in a special sense, revolutionary. The Meiji restoration encapsulates the notion. But such a view was not peculiar to Asia. It had not been uncommon in Renaissance Europe: indeed the concept of renaissance is not incompatible with it. Machiavelli's *Discorsi* may itself have been recapturing the attitude of the Romans, and his own *Il Principe* did not follow the same pattern. But something of the same approach was evident in the English Revolution. It aimed to restore the time past.

> every age
> Appears to souls who live every age in't (ask Carlyle)
> Most unheroic. Ours, for instance, ours...
> A pewter age – mixed metal, silver-washed;
> An age of scum, spooned off the richer past.
> [E. B. Browning, *Aurora Leigh*]

Nonetheless a more linear view of time had begun to prevail. Time could now be saved and wasted. The idea of progress, the subject of a book by J. B. Bury, *The Idea of Progress*,[6] overlaid and reinforced it. The French revolutionaries decided that a new era had started, Year 1. Even those countries that counted by regnal years accepted that their history was a lineal one, moving from Rama III to Rama IV, or indeed from Meiji to Taisho. Sir John Plumb proclaimed in 1963 that 'if there is one idea that makes sense of history, it is the idea of progress... The world is less savage, less brutal, less tyrannical than it was one hundred years ago.'[7]

Reigns have yet remained useful to historians, as labels, as characterising descriptions, such as the Victorian Era. An alternative is to use Christian centuries. Perhaps it was only in the last one that the end of the century was associated with decadence, '*fin de siècle*', 'a kind of decimal determinism'.[8] Sometimes centuries are stretched to suit, for example, Braudel's long sixteenth or Hobsbawm's short twentieth.

If most mortals like to break up time, writers have to. How are 'abridgments' otherwise to be made manageable? Butterfield asked. 'The difficulty of the general historian is that he has to abridge and that he must do it without altering the meaning and the peculiar message of history...'[9] Things have to be left out: but abridgment must not do violence to the complexity of the historical process. Too often, text book writers were at fault, compiling indeed from other abridgments. Abridgment had to maintain the 'texture' of history.[10]

More recently, French historians have attempted an alternative approach, splitting time, as it were, horizontally rather than vertically. 'For Braudel, time, like Gaul or the Almighty, could be divided into three parts... The short-term produced the "event", the middling the "conjuncture", and from the long duration came the "structure".'[11]

Both approaches, vertical and horizontal, have their dangers. What may seem the convenience of the first can be an inconvenience. If the historian is seeking explanations, they will not be readily confined within a chronological framework. Even in a single state, changes are sure to be too complex to be aptly related to the activities of even the strongest monarch. If the century has to be compressed or stretched, what validity has it as a descriptor or a divider?

The second approach risks imbalance in the relationship of the long-term and the contingent. It may underplay the events – often political – in favour of the continuities, and diminish the political, even though the political may be part of the context. It is a guide to thinking about the problems of writing history. But it can be as inadequate as a 'narrative' can be.

Both approaches, of course, are tied to prescriptions about what is significant or important that has occurred over time. '...periods are modes of dealing with specific questions and must change with the questions',

Anthony Reid has declared.[12] Adopting a time-frame may be the result of a decision as to what is important, or it may lead to a decision as to what is important. Writing a general text is likely to fall into the first category. The problem is to do that without falling, or appearing to fall, into the second.

The only valid approach is perhaps what might be called the 'health warning' approach. Bear in mind the nature of the historiographical enterprise. No book offers the final word. No structure will comprise the whole mansion. No explanation will be complete. No time-lines will do justice to a story that has a beginning but no beginning and an end but no end.

If these are counsels for a singly authored work, they are even more difficult to apply to a multi-authored one. Such may have to be divided volume from volume, as well as contribution from contribution. Contribution may be divided from contribution by content as well as time-frame. There will be no answer appropriate to all the topics, let alone one that satisfies all the authors or all their readers. The editor will be criticised; haunted, too, by the fear that decisions that had to be arbitrary have become the guiding principles, if not of the authors, then of the students and the teachers who use the work in first coming to terms with the history or histories concerned.

In the 1950s and 1960s, when independent states had just been set up or were being set up, there was a concern, too, to decolonise historiography. John Bastin and his critics discussed the 'Western element' in Southeast Asian historiography, and John Smail conceived of 'autonomous' histories. At times the contending parties went too far. 'Taken to the extreme, autonomous histories that push the colonizers or their elite collaborators into the shadows would produce the same distortions as do colonial histories that push the "natives" or subaltern groups into the shadows', as Laurie Sears has recognised.[13]

The historians of several Southeast Asian states are now concerned to write 'national' history. What that might be is a subject of much discussion in the profession. Is it a history designed to serve a 'national' purpose? That seems to be one facet of it, and the search for a book or books that might be used in schools and in junior university courses seems to point that way. For some, however, it goes further than that. It is an assertion that history cannot be written by other than 'nationals' and can only be written in the 'national' language. That case has been put strongly by some of the historians at the University of the Philippines and by others in Thailand and in Brunei Darussalam. It represents in some sense a recrudescence of views that were common in the decolonisation period of the 1950s and 1960s. Now 'decolonisation' is not at issue, but 'globalisation' may be. Nations not only seek to boost their unity, but also their distinctiveness. The 'global village' is not in prospect. Or if it is, each house will have assertively different architecture and its own garden to cultivate.

Edward Said has expressed his concern. 'If one believes with Gramsci that an intellectual vocation is socially possible as well as desirable, then it is an inadmissible contradiction at the same time to build analyses of historical experience around exclusions that stipulate, for instance, that only women can understand feminine experience, only Jews can understand Jewish suffering, only formerly colonial subjects can understand colonial experience.'[14]

An historian may well wonder where this places the profession that has emerged, in Europe, in the US, in Australasia, in Southeast Asia itself, in the twentieth century. Writing textbooks is bound, as Butterfield put it, to 'foreshorten' history: indeed he argues that the mechanics of the task ensured the adoption of what he called a Whig interpretation. 'Presentism' is certainly a danger. How is the historian going to structure, to periodise, to resource, the history of a country the frontiers of which may be only recent, the heroes of which may have fought each other, the cultures of which are diverse? It is, after all, striking how few satisfactory histories there are of that strange agglomeration, the UK. It could not have a 'unified historiography', J. G. A. Pocock has argued.[15] Is there not a tendency to write the history of Britain as if it were the history of England? How indeed is the history of Scotland and of Wales to be part of a 'national' history?

'Too close a concern with the remembered past of the various Indonesian peoples always threatened to endanger rather than confirm the newly defined unity', Tony Reid has observed in respect of the history-writing of the early revolution.[16] The structural problems for the historian must also lead to a questioning of the political purpose. If that is to create a sense of nationhood, it is necessary to ask if it is to be a history of the predominant element in the modern state. Might not a sense of belonging be best ensured by a national history at once more subtle and more inclusive?

Nor is the notion that 'national' history is 'nationalised' history a happy thought. It is true that overwhelmingly the history of England has been written by the English and that of the US by Americans. But the insights of others have often been profoundly helpful. Could English history of the eighteenth century ever be the same after Lewis Namier? Does not Paul Kennedy tell us something of the US?

There is a political issue here, too. Nations will have to live with nations, rather than furiously rage together. Assertive national histories will prejudice such a prospect. A sense of nationhood is after all born of knowing others as well as oneself.

The writing of the history of Southeast Asia, and of countries within Southeast Asia, has advanced immeasurably, if irregularly, since the war. It has been stimulated not only by political change and by the expansion of education. Its own controversies have also been stimulating. New evidence has been made available. New approaches have been adopted. It has been a world-wide endeavour, not merely a national one. Surely it has been the better for that. The approach of Braudel to the Mediterranean past inspired the New Zealander/Australian Tony Reid to tackle the Age of Commerce in Southeast Asia. He was no doubt inspired, too, by the relevance of that age of commerce to the present one.

Like the present author, Professor Reid adopted a regional approach. That also is controversial. What relationship do the individual states have to their neighbours? In what sense, if any, do their peoples see themselves as Southeast Asian? The historiographical issues that the concept raises are again both a reflection of the contemporary issues and a contribution to the discussion of them. ●

---

1   Thomas Mann, *The Magic Mountain*, London: Minerva, ch. 5.

2   B. Andaya, *To Live as Brothers*, Honolulu: Hawaii University Press, 1993, p. 8.

3   Lucian W. Pye, *Politics, Personality and Nation Building*, New Haven: Yale University Press, 1962, p. 167.

4   B. Andaya, p. 11.

5   B. Andaya, p. 112.

6   J. B. Bury, *The Idea of Progress* [1921], New York: Macmillan, 1932.

7   J. H. Plumb, *Sunday Times Weekly Review*, 10 March 1963.

8   D. Lowenthal, *The Past is a Foreign Country*, Cambridge: Cambridge University Press, 1985, p. 221.

9   H. Butterfield, *The Whig Interpretation of History*, London: Bell, p. 22.

10 p. 103.

11 R. J. B. Bosworth, *Explaining Auschwitz and Hiroshima*, London and New York: Routledge, 1993, p. 105.

12 A. Reid, *Southeast Asia in the Age of Commerce*, New Haven: Yale University Press, 1993, II, p. xiv.

13 Laurie J. Sears, *Autonomous Histories, Particular Truths*, Madison: Center for Southeast Asian Studies, University of Wisconsin, 1993, pp. 17–18.

14 *Culture and Imperialism*, New York: Knopf, 1993, p. 31.

15 *American Historical Review*, 87.2 (April 1982), p. 331.

16 A. Reid in A. Reid and David Marr, eds, *Perceptions of the Past in Southeast Asia*, Singapore: Heinemann, 1979, pp. 297–8.

SEPTENTRIONALISM

Discourse analysts and deconstructionists, though they may have been destructive in some respects, have been constructive in others. They have stressed that truth, like beauty, lies in the eye of the beholder. Historians have long accepted that different interpretations arise from different viewpoints, and that one person's fact will be another's fiction. They have accepted relativism, though they would mostly not push it to the sterile extremes adopted by those disciplines that appear to have come to it recently and adopted the notion with the passion of the newly converted. It may, after all, be possible that post-modernism is itself only a passing phase, offering a concept that may cast light but not provide the only illumination.

Those who have worked on the history of Southeast Asia have long been aware that the material they have to work with is not only scanty, but slanted. Recent historians have shown that it is necessary, but also possible, to work 'against the grain' of received accounts. What do chronicles tell us? What do colonial records tell us? It is possible to make more of both by juxtaposing both, as the Andayas have shown. Out of archives originally collected for another purpose, James Warren has been able to reconstruct the lives of Sulu pirates and their captives, of Singapore rickshaw coolies, of the prostitutes who were part of Japan's earliest export drive. The challenges are often difficult, and authors themselves rarely feel they have surmounted them. But they, and their readers, usually feel they have come nearer a truthful account, even if it is not the only one. Not believing that a final truth can be reached does not invalidate attempts to get nearer it, nor suggest that all the attempts are equally valid or equally inadequate.

It is certainly true, if one may be allowed to offer so bold a statement without its being itself subject to deconstruction, that, in general, viewpoints shift and, more particularly, that the imperialist phase privileged a kind of discourse from which it was difficult to escape. The long European connexion with Southeast Asia, even though it was irregular and spasmodic, tended to support a colonial view, and even to encourage Europeans to see its earlier history as if it were but a fragment of the history of its great neighbours. To see Southeast Asia for itself, and its people for themselves, was difficult. But imperial officials in fact made serious and partially successful efforts to break away from the conceptual framework of imperialism. Critics like George Orwell, J. S. Furnivall and Victor Purcell emerged within the system, even within a single mind, like Hugh Clifford's. The study of the Indonesian past enjoined upon officials in Netherlands India, though it began as a means to better control, led to a recognition of its autonomy. The most startling case is that of J. C. van Leur, his Weberian sociological approach undermining the entrenched colonial historiography of his fellow Dutchmen.[1]

Indeed the 'Orientalism' of which Edward Said has so influentially written has perhaps never dominated the historiography of Southeast Asia as it has in his view that of the Middle East, or perhaps the Sub-Continent or the Far East. The diversity of the region perhaps stood in the way. So, perhaps paradoxically, did the long European connexions with it. The early years were rarely marked by a sense of total incomprehension or total alienation. The fact that it was difficult to see Southeast Asia as a whole perhaps made it easier to see parts of it clearly.

Seeing it as part of Asia as a whole might lead, however, to a kind of orientalism, and diversity could lead that way, too, if it prompted an impatient bafflement easily amalgamated with contempt, and a disposition to aggregate that magnified the chance of misunderstanding. The counterpart of such confrontation is a reversal of roles: what seemed incomprehensible becomes the only truth; what seemed a source of fear becomes the only source of comfort. Some who are not Asian decide they are; some with a culture of their own devalue it and thus devalue all.

The present author has ventured to use the agglomerant words 'West' or 'Western'. They are a shorthand also easy to misread, sometimes too easy. 'If one of the continuing villainies of imperialism has been located in an inherited European rhetoric which racially essentializes and reduces the colonized ("the Malay"), I cannot fight it or partly distance myself from it', writes Susan Morgan, '... through a rhetoric which essentializes and reduces the would-be colonizers ("British imperialism" or "the British colonial/ imperial perspective").'[2]

Allan Patience criticised *The Voice of Asia* by Mahathir Mohamad and Shintaro Ishihara[3] in yet bolder phrases. 'The "Asian values" they evangelise are echoes of imperial manners, making Mahathir and Ishihara pathetic compradors of a passé neo-colonialism... Their idea of the "West" is tendentious, a reversal of Said's "Orientalism"... Maybe we need a book on *Occidentalism* – which would demonstrate how some "Asian" leaders are trying to construct an idealised account of the "West" to parody it for political purposes.'[4] It is partly in such a context that the present author has suggested yet another perspective. But that cannot be what, but for its unpronounceability, he would be tempted to label Septentrionalism.

Australia and New Zealand have shared only a slight part of their history with the islands and mainland to the north. Australia's contacts even with the Malay peoples were few, New Zealand's nil. The Dutch named New

Holland and New Zealand, but their real concern was with their monopoly in Maluku. In the late eighteenth century, as both areas were embraced by British naval power, a more positive connexion between Southeast Asia and 'Austral-Asia' seemed possible. But subsequent migrations to the antipodean colonies produced a severance rather than a development of contacts with Asia. The Australians became interested in Philippines sugar, in North Borneo timber, in Malayan tin. But contacts with Europe, or rather with Britain, predominated, and it was in relation to them, or in reaction from them, that the Australasian colonies rather self-consciously sought an individuality that they were unspectacularly acquiring in any case. The assignment of Southeast Asia to a number of colonial powers, though largely under the umbrella of the British, further insulated it from Australia and New Zealand, just as it added to the area's own internal division.

In the early twentieth century changes were in preparation; but the revolution came with the Second World War. The decline of British preponderance, the independence of India, the Communist triumph in China, created, in the context of a world struggle for power, a new environment for relations between Australia and New Zealand and Southeast Asia. Within Southeast Asia the colonial regimes were displaced, one by one, by independent regimes, which had to face crucial economic, social and political problems. Australia now had quite different and apparently unstable neighbours and, with the resolution of the West Irian question, acquired a common frontier with the most populous and powerful of them. New Zealand, more remote, remained more isolated. But a reshaping of the policies of both dominions seemed essential: a reappraisal, too, of popular attitudes; and, on both grounds, the introduction of educational programmes, designed to bridge the intellectual and emotional gap created by the distinctive histories of Southeast Asia and Austral-Asia.

Attempting these tasks meant facing the emotional obstacles that the imperialist past had left the Australians and New Zealanders. Asia was something large, composite, difficult to understand, mysteriously combining wealth and poverty. The apprehension was sharpened, particularly in the case of Australia, by a sense of proximity, a sense of vulnerability. 'What Great Britain calls the Far East', as R. G. Menzies put it in 1939, 'is to us the near north'.[5] And the British were no longer able to sustain the status quo that had offered security.

The relationship became both more complex and more positive in the postwar years. In part that was the result of economic trends. While Britain joined the EEC, the Japanese economy boomed and the 'Tigers' emerged. Without abandoning economic relationships with other parts of the world, Australia and New Zealand became more involved with the changes in what was now called the Pacific Rim. The revolutions in transport and communication tended, not only to diminish distance, but to enhance contact.

The contact was personal, too: students and tourists went to and came from Asian countries, as did officials and businessmen. Substantial migrations have followed. That, however, only posed the problem of the relationship with Asia in new forms.

There were two reactions at the extremes. One was the view that Australia and New Zealand were themselves part of Asia. Some insisted, in reversal from an early separation, that they were, after all, 'Asian' and others might use the larger rhetoric to describe what in effect was a smaller change. 'Australasia' indeed meant 'southern Asia', not, as some had seemed to think, a kind of Australian dominance over the Tasman. But the real meaning behind the name might be no more accurate than the meaning previously given it. The second reaction was 'Septentrionalism'. 'Asia' was viewed from the Far South as a whole. Of it the observers in general felt that they were not part, even that it was 'the other'. What these two views had in common, perhaps, was a tendency to see Asia through antipodean eyes. That might distort it. It would obscure its real character by diminishing or exaggerating the differences between Far North and Far South, continuing to lump the Asians together, and either lumping in the Australasians or lumping them out. The view from the South could, however, add a new perspective, and a valid one.

Public discussion in Australia and New Zealand has often addressed Asia as a market, latterly as a region about which the community in general, and especially the business community, should be more 'literate'. In both cases, and in others, the label should carry a warning. 'Asia' is not a unity, nor does it see itself as such. In a world of nationalisms and internationalisms, Australians and New Zealanders should think not of Asia, but of Japan, of China, of India, of Indonesia, of the Philippines, Singapore, and Malaysia, of Burma, Thailand, Vietnam and Cambodia. Doing otherwise will not be appreciated, nor will it promote 'literacy' about them. The British are sensitive about being called Europeans, the Japanese about being called Asians. Do Australians and New Zealanders like to be called Australasians?

They should question, too, the hyphenated linking, Asia-Pacific. Traffic among the countries along the shores of the Pacific may be growing, but to understand their future, and indeed the prospects of that traffic, their diversity must be recognised: look, not only to the Asia-Pacific, but to the Asia-specific. The development of APEC, with its emphasis on trade facilitation perhaps leading to trade liberalisation, is starting to make some sense of the concept of the Asia-Pacific region. But progress will be slow, and diversity will remain the region's most obvious characteristic.

There is a risk, too, in going the other way, of sinking the identities of Australia and New Zealand in an amorphous 'Asian' or 'Asia-Pacific' mass. Some of the rhetoric of New Zealand's 'ASIA 2000' programme, though by no means all, headed in this direction. In their anxiety to awaken New

Zealanders to the 'reality' of Asia, opinion-makers sometimes incautiously told them they were 'part of the greater Asian region', or were themselves Asian. That was as mistaken as it was unwise. It was unwise because, an over-reaction itself, it produced another over-reaction. New Zealanders did not consider themselves Asian, and quite reasonably so. As the Foreign Minister, Don McKinnon, has said, 'this initiative to assert our place in Asia does not mean removing history or our heritage. New Zealand's unique identity is an important plus as we seek to enhance our relations with the Asian Region'. 'Asians' indeed did not see New Zealanders' endeavours to be viewed as Asian as convincing. What the aim should properly be is to assert an identity as New Zealanders, anxious to be informed about Asian countries, to deal with them state-to-state and people-to-people and economy-to-economy.

In the consideration of the issues and in bringing them before a wider public, the universities clearly had a major role to play. Characteristically they had been centred on the study of European cultures. Now new material was to be introduced, so as at once to arouse and to satisfy the interest of their students. The universities were also to do what they could to help the community as a whole adjust to the changed situation. If possible, too, they had to help respond to the challenges facing Southeast Asian scholarship: major gaps had to be filled, major revisions undertaken. In facing them Australians and New Zealanders were not without certain advantages. It might be that Australians and New Zealanders could free themselves of European terminologies and chronologies without flying to anti-colonial extremes, and so contribute to a better all-round understanding of Southeast Asian history. If the shortness of their history and the tightness of their British connexion committed Australians to some sort of love-hate relationship with European influences, this itself could help them to understand the attitudes of Indonesian intellectuals to the Dutch legacy. Australians and New Zealanders shared apprehensions of China with some Southeast Asian countries. But they might be especially fitted, in view of their own background, to understand the nature of the Chinese community in Southeast Asia: not a community drawn from the upper classes of its homeland, but none the less loyal to its culture. Belonging themselves to small nations, without a substantial imperialist history, students from Australia and New Zealand might recognise the importance in Southeast Asia of the doctrines of nationality and self-determination, of the aspirations of the new states or 'nations'.

Over the past thirty or more years the universities of the Far South, particularly those in Australia, have made major contributions to the understanding of Southeast Asia. They have not only served their national communities; they have also contributed to the scholarly world in even more ways than the hopeful anticipated. At a time when the study of Southeast

Asia was waning in the old colonial territories, and the interest in the US rose and fell, the contribution of the Australians, all the more assiduous, was all the more necessary. It is not part of Asia, but it may be the place where parts of Asia are being best studied.

Ruth McVey predicts 'a continuing internationalization' of Southeast Asian studies. 'Eventually, we should expect the emergence of a planetary system in which various foreign centres of research orbit around a Southeast Asia which is their powerful source of analysis as well as of study material.' That, however, may take a long time, given the 'regnant paradigm', and its focus on modernisation and the nation-state. No alternative vision has emerged, as she adds, but the very lack of it may leave the way open for creative scholarship.[6]

The present book does not seek to escape the 'regnant paradigm' by resort to other disciplines or theoretical approaches. The author does, however, suggest that setting the emergence of the modern states of Southeast Asia in a larger context could at once also challenge that paradigm and contribute to an understanding of what is currently called 'globalisation'. ●

---

1   J. C. van Leur, *Indonesian Trade and Society*, The Hague and Bandung: van Hoeve, 1955, Foreword, pp. v–vi.

2   Susan Morgan, *Place Matters*, New Brunswick: Rutgers University Press, 1996, p. 9.

3   Mahathir Mohamad and Shintaro Ishihara, *The Voice of Asia: Two leaders discuss the coming century*, trans. I. Baldwin, Tokyo: Kodansha, 1995.

4   *Campus Review*, 28/3–3/4/96.

5   Broadcast, 26/4/39. *Documents on Australian Foreign Policy*, vol. 2, p. 98.

6   Ruth McVey, 'Change and Continuity in Southeast Asian Studies', *Journal of South East Asian Studies*, 26, 1 (March 1995), p. 9.

INDEX